ISLANDS OF INCARCERATION

Seven Authors

by

Editors

John Pearn

Peggy Carter

Published by:
Boolarong Press
38/1631 Wynnum Road
Tingalpa Qld 4173
Australia.
www.boolarongpress.com.au

First published by Amphion Press 1995
Second published by Boolarong Press in 2020

A catalogue record for this book is available from the National Library of Australia

ISBN: 9781925877403 (paperback)

Cover design by Boolarong Press (cover photo's courtesy of the State Libary of WA, the History Council of NSW and the Tasmania Government)

Printed and bound by Watson Ferguson & Company, Tingalpa, Australia

Contents

ACKNOWLEDGEMENTS

BOOK OF THIS NATURE CAN ONLY BE produced with the encouragement of many friends. The Editors and Authors thank especially the following colleagues who have made this work possible —

Nestle Foods, whose support of the welfare of children and adolescents is much appreciated; and in particular Miss Julie-Ann Okely and Mr P Kumarasinghe for much encouragement.

Glaxo Australia for continued help and support; and in particular Mr Ian Munro, Queensland Manager.

We thank also the extended White, Carter and Pearn families for material support.

Many colleagues and organizations have helped with research; with scholastic encouragement; with the kind provision of drawings and sketches; and with gracious permission to publish photographs, illustrations and related material from archives, museums and libraries, for which special thanks. In particular we acknowledge the support of —

The State Library of New South Wales, the Mitchell Library (State Library of New South Wales), the Archives Authority of New South Wales, and Mr Geoffrey Chapman Ingleton for their kind support and permission to publish sketches and rare archives;

The Allport Library and Museum of Fine Arts, Hobart,
The Tasmanian Archives Office,
Mr Reginald Graham of Queenstown and Strahan,
Nucolorvue of Devonport, all of Tasmania;

Mrs Mary Duke of Norfolk Island
The Royal Historical Society of Queensland
Mr Mark Harris, Mrs Lynne Packer,
Ms Alison Corcoran, Miss Maryanne Wade and
Professor Gael Phillips of Brisbane;

The Rottnest Island Authority and Museum, The Library Board of Western Australia, and Dr Robert Pearce AM, RFD, all of Perth.

In particular we thank also the Committee of the International Conference of Medical History, "Mutiny and Medicine" of the Australian Society of the History of Medicine, for their confidence and support.

Professor John Pearn AM, RFD
Mrs Peggy Carter OAM

Amphion Press
Department of Child Health
University of Queensland
Australia

NOTES ON CONTRIBUTORS

Dr Peter Burns is a general medical practitioner of Perth, Western Australia. After graduation in medicine he served at Fremantle (1956) and at Meekatharra in Western Australia (1957). He served as a Staff Specialist with the Royal Air Force in Britain and in Germany (1963 – 1968). He has special interests in the history of medicine and its evolution in Australia

Mrs Peggy Carter OAM is the co-editor and co-publisher of Amphion Press, a non-profit publishing unit within the Department of Child Health at the University of Queensland in Brisbane — a publishing unit dedicated to the promotion of research and the dissemination of the history of health and its development in Australia. She has contributed much to the encouragement and promotion of voluntary writing groups.

Ms Jeanette Covacevich AM is the senior Curator of Vertebrates at the Queensland Museum, in Brisbane. An historian, scientist and writer, she is the President of the Royal Society of Queensland and a former President of the Australian Society of Herpetologists. A noted ecologist, she is the author of many papers and reports on the heritage of the natural environment and on the humankind-environment interface.

Dr John Duke AM is a retired consultant physician and historian, of Norfolk Island. He was Staff Specialist within the Department of Public Health in Lae, Papua New Guinea (1961 – 1965); and has worked in senior staff positions at the Commonwealth Serum Laboratories and at the Preston and Northcote Hospital in Melbourne. He has been the Consultant Physician to the Norfolk Island Hospital since 1988.

The Honourable Justice Michael Kirby AC, CMG, is the President of the Court of Appeal, The Supreme Court of New South Wales, in Sydney. A noted judge, speaker and writer he has served as a Member of the Executive Committee of the International Commission of Jurists since 1989 and has been Chairman since 1992. He was Chairman of the Law Reform Commission of Australia (1975 – 1984); and has served as Chancellor of Macquarie University since 1984.

Mr Peter Ludlow is a senior pharmacist with Queensland Health, based in the Pharmacy Department of the Princess Alexandra Hospital, in Brisbane. An historian and author, he has published works on the history of quarantine; and on the history of Moreton Bay in Queensland.

Sister Catherine O'Carrigan is a nun and member of the Order of the Sisters of Charity based at Potts Point in Sydney. A professional historian, she is a former teacher of history and art; and for more than two decades has been the official historian to St Vincent's Hospital, Sydney. She has made special contributions to the history of religious and charitable bodies and their part in the evolution of health care in Australia.

Professor John Pearn AM, RFD, is the Professor of Child Health at the University of Queensland. An historian and writer, he is the author of more than 100 papers and books on the history of health in Australia. He is Vice President of both the Royal Historical Society of Queensland and of the Australian Society of the History of Medicine.

Dr Brian Reid is a general medical practitioner of Rapid Creek, near Darwin in the Northern Territory. He is a foundation Councillor of the Australian Society of the History of Medicine and has special interests in the evolution of health care in northern Australia.

FOREWORD

he inhabitants of the British isles were long regarded by the inhabitants of the European continent as particularly uncivilised in the matter of criminal punishment. Their ingenuity in devising new sanctions for those convicted of criminal offences had few equals on the Continent. Hanging, drawing and quartering was particularly gruesome. Chaining pirates to die in the tides of the Thames was thought exquisitely appropriate to a sea-faring nation. Capital and corporal punishment were exported to a great Empire. Indeed, Australia itself began, in a sense, as a great island of incarceration. Had not the American colonies and settlements been lost in the Revolution of 1776, with consequent loss of places to which prisoners could be exported from England it is doubtful that the English settlement of Australia would ever have ensued. How different the history of this continent might have been if Governor Phillip had not been sent here to establish the incarceration settlement at Botany Bay.

In a sense, therefore, the modern history of Australia is the product of penal decisions taken by distracted administrators at Whitehall concerning how they could rid themselves of unwanted prisoners and put them on an island far away. Such islands have long held a fascination for prison administrators.

The passage of intervening water gives a feeling of security. Nature provides, with economy, the isolation which it would otherwise cost a great deal to achieve. The island becomes a symbol of exclusion. It has been so from ancient times. It has been so in different cultural traditions, as Devil's Island (of France) and Alcatraz (of the United States) tell us in countless books and popular movies, their exotic tales.

The reality was often much less romantic, as the essays in this book demonstrate. If Sydney Harbour, to which the hapless prisoners under Governor Phillip's care were soon transferred, seemed a long way from the civilised world, it was a gentle and beguiling place in comparison to the islands of incarceration, established around the Australian continent. These were places for the despatch of particularly difficult prisoners. Imagine the sinking feeling of a prisoner committed to Sarah Island in Macquarie Harbour at the extremity of Van Diemen's Land

... the most wretched outpost ...

as it was called, in the British Empire. The ruins at Norfolk Island bear witness to the establishment of the successive penal regimes on that remote island. Captain James Cook had discovered Norfolk Island in October 1774. How astonishing it is that Governor Phillip, but a week after the raising of the Union flag at Sydney Cove, despatched the Supply to establish settlement on Norfolk, later to be used as a place of banishment for the worst type of convict.

The primitive conditions of the islands described in this book and the cruelty of many of the officials are only softened by the tales of dutiful magistrates, attentive medicos, the occasional enlightened official (such as Alexander Maconochie of Norfolk) and the spirit of the convicts. The provision of formal medical assistance was usually missing. Typical was the case of the dispenser on Cockatoo Island in Sydney Harbour whose qualifications could not be checked because he claimed to have lost them. Yet he kept a valuable record. It is the source of detailed knowledge of the variety of medical conditions not unsurprisingly suffered in the unhealthy environments.

It is the lesson of the law, that we understand the wrongs of today by examining the errors of our past. The common law, that great gift which came with the prisoners on the First Fleet from England is itself a record of wrongs done, sometimes righted. In that sense, lawyers are always the prisoners of the past. But one hopes that they are thinking prisoners and with spirit — ever ready learn from mistakes and to correct them in the to learn from mistakes and to correct them in the name of justice.

This work, published for the Australian Society of the History of Medicine, is to be welcomed for the light which it throws upon thy errors of earlier times and for the lessons which it presents about the constant struggle between penal policies of retribution and enlightenment.

We should not congratulate ourselves too much on the progress we have made in the intervening years. True, the islands of incarceration described in this book have been closed. But on the big island Australia, there are still places of incarceration which are extremely primitive and conditions which are distinctly unhealthy. Now, we have new problems, such as the potential peril of HIV/AIDS in our prisons. We need new Maconochies to insist upon enlightenment and to ensure the protection of the life and dignity of the prisoners, whilst they remain in the care of the state.

In Parliament, penal policies constantly swing on the pendulum of perceived public opinion. It often responds to the community's anxiety about crime, spurred on by alarmist media reports such as produced, in panic, the Community Protection Act 1994 (NSW). In a recent decision by my Court, *Kable v Director of Public Prosecutions* New South Wales Court of Appeal, unreported, 9 May 1995, that measure was described by the judges as constituting

> ... an infringement of a fundamental human right

and "a dangerous precedent [which] opens the door to the possibility of abuse". So in 1995, our enlightenment is far from complete. We can learn for the future from a study of the wrongs of the present and the past. If any country on earth should do so, it should be Australia, given the way our modern government arose and flourished around the islands of incarceration.

The Hon. Justice Michael Kirby AC, CMG
President, The Court of Appeal, The Supreme Court, Sydney, N.S. W.

INTRODUCTION

n enlightened, modern world sees criminal sentencing as combining not only the elements of punishment, deterrence and protection of the public, but also those of expatiation, compensation, reform and rehabilitation. All who are involved particularly with youth would wish to see the efficient return of an erstwhile offender, albeit reformed, to society as a useful and contributing member of the general population.

By the twenty-first century, a minority of nations still do not include compensation, reform and rehabilitation as the core of their penal systems. Some one in thirty of all males, even in the most enlightened and wealthy of Western societies, are “unfavourably known to the police”. Societal approach to such wrong-doers has, in the relatively recent span of the last two centuries, been a changing one. It has been one of experiment and of a gradual, perhaps enlightened change with an emphasis on humanitarian treatment of the fallen in society. The change in mind-set from retribution to reform, as society’s prime approach to its criminal element, is a recent phenomenon even in those enlightened societies which espouse rehabilitation as a core tenet.

One of the prime components of all former penal systems has been that of imprisonment or incarceration. In its most extreme form this has meant banishment "beyond the city wall". The concept of exile or banishment from society is older than recorded history itself. In bronze age times exclusion from the city precincts was the lot of the chronically ill — such as the unfortunate sufferers from leprosy or Hansen's Disease — rather than criminals who were dealt with in other ways.

Transportation of criminals beyond national boundaries — out of sight, out of mind — did not develop until the early eighteenth century. Its equivalent, however — sentencing criminals to be galley slaves or to serve in armies or navies operating beyond a country's boundaries — such was in effect a functional exile. In 1717, the first *Transportation Act* was passed in England. It stated that —

> ... the labour of criminals in the Colonies would benefit the Nation.

The first transported convicts from England were, in fact, slaves. The Government sold convicted felons to shipping contractors who in turn were required to post bonds of their guaranteed safe delivery to Virginia in America. When the purchased convicts arrived in the American colonies, they were then resold to American colonists, for a going rate in the order of £20 per convict. This system proved admirable in that England rid herself of criminals and at the same time recouped the cost of their incarceration prior to transportation. The colonists obtained white slaves to work in the cotton fields, to work as servants in the houses of the more affluent and in the case of educated convicts, to work as servants in business.

Opposition to this system came initially not from those with humanitarian considerations, but from concepts that white supremacy was being compromised by the "shipping out" of white slaves. Convicts started to accumulate in English gaols, engendering the great humanitarian advocacy of reformers such as John Howard.

Prison hulks, particularly those on the Thames, became overcrowded and typhus (gaol fever) became rampant. After the defeat of the British Forces in the American War of Independence of 1776, transportation ceased and the problem of what to do with convicted felons became acute. Australia was one solution.

France established colonies of criminals as micro-societies of the permanently or semi-permanently banished in Africa, at New Caledonia and at Devil's Island off French Guiana. Russia established exile penal colonies in Siberia, a system greatly expanded and refined with deadly efficiency under the twentieth century Stalinist regimes. All these outpost colonies, by their remoteness, by their self-contained isolation and surrounded by the natural barriers of the sea, desert, permafrost or jungle — all formed in effect, islands of incarceration.

Prisons in the sense that the world knows them today are a relatively recent phenomenon, dating from the 1700s. Their antecedents were the dungeons of medieval times; and later the workhouses and houses of correction of London, the latter first established in 1557. Other such predecessors of today's prisons were gaols such as the Debtors' Prison and the hulks of ships established on the River Thames. A hulk as a floating "Island of Incarceration" for delinquent boys was still operating on the Brisbane River at Fort Lytton in Queensland in the 1870s. The concept of an island prison was used effectively by pirate captains and by mutineers.

The workhouses and "Houses of Correction" of England and the gaols established in river-tethered hulks replaced the galleys, mutilation, slavery, the stocks and capital punishment as society's response to criminal behaviour. Those prisons of the eighteenth century differed from modern prisons in that there was little segregation by age or sex; and that the emphasis was totally on punishment or retribution. An important functional difference was that the gaolers of those early prisons were dependent for their living on fees paid by the prisoners or their dependents.

An off-shore, prison island satisfied several perceived requirements of the time. Punishment and retribution, often of a particularly severe kind, was one essential element. Banishment and exile further extended the concept of punishment, but also removed from the eyes of normal citizens the ever-present reminder of the small step to criminal behaviour inherent in many.

The concept of banishment is not illogical. If one offends against a democratically elected and governed society, one is rejecting the ethos of that society. In a logical sense, one thus loses the right to remain part of it. Thus France's concept of Devil's Island was to establish an alternative society for those who had rejected the mores of mainland France. Such in itself is in no way illogical. In this sense, all prisons are essentially islands of incarceration. The fact that a prison is situated on a real island instead of being a compound tastefully screened by trees or natural features in a city or town is incidental in this context.

Prison islands consisting of real islands surrounded by sea, introduce two extra elements — one real and one potential. The first is that the offender is seen to be truly banished as an exile, and thus is functionally deprived of visitation by family and friends. Physical contact, such as with the inmates of Devil's Island Port Arthur or Melville Island off the northern Australian coast, was thus impossible.

The second theme inherent in island prisons is an implicit one. The implication is that contact,

supervision and punishment will be outside the day-to-day jurisdiction of a higher monitoring authority. In decades and centuries past, such brought the potential for special abuses. It also engendered a special trepidation, often a realistic one, amongst would-be or convicted villains that the punishment component of their sentences would be the more severe. Without doubt, the establishment of island prisons was undertaken in an attempt to increase the efficiency of prison as a deterrent for those contemplating crime.

Reform in prison systems began in the early nineteenth century and followed two parallel streams. The first of these was the development of a more "efficient" system whereby a wrongdoer would reflect on his or her crimes and hopefully, following release, would not re-offend. Experiments began using "separatist" (or the Philadelphia System) incarceration of prisoners. Such a system was in effect solitary confinement and is a system still used in exceptional cases in many Western prisons today; and continues as a routine form of convict management in many nations. An alternative experiment employed the "silent" (or the Auburn System), named following the building in 1825 of the Auburn Penitentiary in New York.

In the Auburn System convicts were allowed to associate physically for supervised work, but were maintained in absolute silence.

Communication between the prisoners was totally forbidden. The ingenuity of prisoners to circumvent this imposed lack of communication is legendary.

A pioneering experiment was conducted at Norfolk Island when Captain Alexander Maconochie developed the "mark system" by which convicts could reduce their sentences by good behaviour, for which they earned marks or credits. This brilliant development — the elements of the parole system — was expanded in France by Bonneville de Marsangy who promoted the practice of conditional release, that is of parole, for good conduct.

From this it was a small step, philosophically, to the concept of occupational training or the encouragement of productive work, as opposed to the punishments of mindless stone-breaking or of shot carrying. Such occupational and rehabilitative training, it was believed, would have a rehabilitative role for the good of the prisoner himself, rather than being simply a means of self-support for the gaol.

The parallel theme in Western societies, in step with these revolutionary rehabilitative trends in penology, was the broad societal move towards a more enlightened humanity. It was an awareness, promoted by a minority of courageous reformers, that there but for the grace of God, go I. This approach to the "offender as a brother", albeit a fallen one in society, had its modern origins in the advocacy of John Howard and in the writings of Charles Dickens. It was a product of its time. It was a glimmering spark alongside similar embers being fanned by Lord Shaftesbury's reforms of working conditions for children; and of Wilberforce's efforts to abolish slavery.

These themes came together in the phenomenon of convict transportation. On the one hand banishment from national borders was punishment akin to execution or total incarceration. The prisoner simply disappeared from society which was protected from his presence and thus from the hurt of any future wrongdoing. On the other hand transportation was more humane than execution.

In many cases the results were the same. One-quarter of the convicts transported on the Second Fleet to Australia, in 1790, died on the voyage and another quarter were dead within two weeks of their arrival at Port Jackson. However, from the prisoner's point of view at the moment of sentencing, it was better to be sent to Moreton Bay, Port Arthur or Norfolk Island rather than to hang the next morning in Newgate Prison in London.

Islands, as places of incarceration, thus formed a place of banishment, of exile and of punishment.

Islands of Incarceration: The narrow Eaglehawk Neck, guarded by a line of soldiers and dogs, made the Tasman Peninsula and its contained Port Arthur, an effective island of incarceration for the worst prisoners. Following the reforms of John Howard in Bedford and of Captain Maconochie at Norfolk Island experiments in reform and rehabilitation were started at Pentonville in London in 1842, with its Model Prison. The Separate System was adopted at Port Arthur, in Van Diemen's Land in 1848. Here fifty of the worst felons lived and worked in total silence and anonymity — without conversation even with warders. This photograph, courtesy of Professor Gael Phillips, shows one such "Silent Cell" of the Separate or Model Prison, which has been preserved.

An enlightened twenty-first century world will emphasise rehabilitation, extirpation and recompense in its dealing with wrongdoers, rather than simple punishment and retribution. Unfortunately, how to achieve this ideal status is still essentially unknown. Recidivist rates remain high even for prisoners released from the most enlightened penal institutions. However, a study of the penal systems of the islands of incarceration of the past will help in defining a clearer path for improvement in the future.

Professor John Pearn
The Australian Society of the History of Medicine

Islands of Incarceration: The Penitentiary and Flour Mill buildings at Port Arthur, in Tasmania. The narrow isthmus of Eaglehawk Neck, guarded by a line of soldiers and dogs, made Port Arthur a functional "island of incarceration". Built in 1848 to accommodate 657 prisoners, it became the final repository for many recidivist prisoners from other penal stations in Australia. Photograph 1989, courtesy of Nucolorvue, Tasmania, with acknowledgements.

Islands of Incarceration: Woody Island in Little Norfolk Bay, south of Eaglehawk Neck, near Port Arthur, Tasmania. Photograph, February 1993, courtesy of Professor John Pearn.

Sarah Island

The infamous prison Island in Macquarie Harbor, Van Diemen Land

John Pearn

he ring of the sentence "For the term of your natural life" held special meaning for those men and women incarcerated on Sarah Island. This small island even today remote, lies in Macquarie Harbour on the west coast of Tasmania. In the first half of the nineteenth century, when for a period of eleven years it was the home at any one time of several hundred men and women convicts, it lay at the limits of the mapped and known world.

Of all the world's prison islands, Sarah Island and its tiny satellite, Grummett Island were the most infamous. Unlike that other famous island of incarceration, Devil's Island off the coast of French Guiana, Sarah Island received primarily recidivist prisoners, and those of the worst type. Unlike St Helena, no ships other than supply ships, and those infrequently, called there. Unlike the Chateau d'If, off the coast of France, the graveyard was not the sea but

an ever growing array of crosses on another satellite, Halliday Island. This latter came to be viewed as a haven of considerable appeal, albeit in death, by the living inmates of Sarah and Grummett Islands incarcerated nearby.

All colonial powers have had to grapple with the problem of recidivist prisoners — those who committed sequential crimes during the servitude of their primary sentence. The ethos of nineteenth century penology was punishment, retribution and deterrence. Reformers such as John Howard, the High Sheriff of Bedfordshire, and Captain Alexander Maconochie (1787 – 1860) of Norfolk Island introduced courageous and in their time, controversial reforms. Maconochie's book, *Thoughts on Convict Management*, further developed his innovations of a "mark system" whereby good behaviour was rewarded and rehabilitation promoted.

These exceptions aside, the concept of rehabilitation and potential re-entry into a free society is very much a twentieth century phenomenon. In the penal colonies in Australia, convicts were classified and segregated according to their behaviour under sentence —

> The convicts were classified in 1826 into seven classes. The first of these ranked immediately below the assigned class and was composed of men of especially good conduct ... road gangs comprised the third class; the fourth consisted of chain gangs ... in 1826 the sixth was the Maria Island (Van Diemen‘s Land) class and the seventh the Macquarie [Harbour] class.[1]

Thus it was to the limits of the known world, to Macquarie Harbour on Tasmania's west coast, that the worst recidivist prisoners were sent. Macquarie Harbour is, in the eyes of today's tourist visitor, a place of rugged beauty and a last bastion of the primeval wilderness of millennia of former ages. Into it flows the Gordon River along whose banks grow great stands of Huon pine which once extended densely along the foreshores of the entire Harbour. It was the potential for logging this timber — "that the prisoners could be put to some productive use" — together with the desolation and remoteness of the site, which held such appeal for colonial authorities in 1822. Within Macquarie Harbour itself, lies Sarah Island and its tiny satellite, Grummett Island also known as Small Island. The islands are relatively infertile and barren in places. The third island, Phillips Island was less infertile and became the site of the Convict

Farm. The entire Macquarie Harbour settlement was to become

> ... the most wretched outpost in the British Empire, hated by its convicts, military and civilian settlers' alike.[2]

The story of its settlement and an account of life on its islands of incarceration, thus brings a perspective to the current and very contemporary issue of the rehabilitation of today's offenders.

SETTLEMENT AT SARAH ISLAND

Macquarie Harbour was established in 1822 by the Governor of Van Diemen's Land William Sorell. Based in Hobart where, in the era before the establishment of Port Arthur, some of the worst prisoners had been sent, Sorell felt himself to be in —

> ... urgent want ... of a local spot of farther punishment, to which The Worst Class of Convicts could be sent, and where their labour would be productive.[3]

This approach was maintained by Sorell's successor, Governor Arthur, who felt that a convict's "whole fate should ... be the very last degree of misery consistent with humanity".[4]

In 1822, Macquarie Harbour with its tiny five-hectare Sarah Island seemed to offer all that could be desired of such an "island of incarceration". It was remote, inhospitable, deemed to be secure from escape and was surrounded by an apparently limitless wilderness of valuable timber whose milling would necessitate hard, yet productive labour.

An Island of Incarceration: Watercolour View of Macquarie Harbour, Van Diemen's Land" by an unknown artist. This painting, circa 1830, shows Sarah Island from the eastern side. No confirmed escapes were ever recorded from this prison island to which were sent convicts of the worst type. The convict establishments, including, the gaol, bakehouse, tannery and Shipyards are to the left of the Boat Basin, the central structure (arrowed) protruding into the Harbour. The signalling Flagstaff is to right. Courtesy of the Allport Library and Museum of Fine Arts, State Library of Tasmania, Hobart, with acknowledgements.

Macquarie Harbour, from the geological and hydrological point of view, is one of the most interesting harbours in the world. It is a vast inland waterway, its connections with the sea being through a turbulent and narrow race less than 100 metres wide, not inappropriately known since the convict days as *Hell's Gates*. The water in the upper reaches of Macquarie Harbour has unique layers of fresh and saline water; and the great mass of tannin-stained water contained in the Harbour can defy the force of the moon's gravitational pull. Thus the tidal race through *Hell's Gates* is not the diurnal ebb and flow of harbour-mouths elsewhere. Rather, atmospheric pressure over the great Southern Ocean is a major controlling force which determines whether water will ebb or flow through the narrow *Hell's Gates* entrance.

This rare and fascinating "atmospheric tide", has no defined periodicity. The great Harbour may ebb with the surging tidal race for many days before the flow stills and is reversed and water re-enters the Harbour. The tidal race can reach twelve knots, faster than a sailing ship or a supply brig could conquer in an effort to enter the Harbour. Such is a source of wonderment for tourists and geographers of today; but such meant that the isolation of the settlements based about Sarah Island thirty kilometres up harbour, was functionally complete. No supply ship could afford to try to ride out the storms on the inhospitable west coast of Tasmania, the prevailing gales always on to a feared lee shore. None could wait without shelter for the unpredictable tides to change such that the ship could seek the safety of the Harbour and bring succour to its inmates —

> Hell's Gate, the narrow entrance to Macquarie Harbour, less than a hundred metres wide (275ft) and choked by a sand bar, which at low tide lay less than 3 metres under water, was always the terror of the mariners. To pass through this

narrow channel was, even with local knowledge, a risky journey. Every care had to be taken to pass through it on the right side. Often whirlpools occurred; with currents running one way on the surface and another way below it.

Ships with urgently needed goods for the settlement often had to seek shelter from the boisterous weather in Recherche Bay. Then, when the weather improved, they were lucky to reach Port Davey. There they usually had to wait again, often for several weeks. Then came the last leg of the voyage. This was the most difficult one, and on many occasions, ships just could not reach Macquarie Harbour and had to return to Port Davey until the westerly winds abated. Ships who reached Cape Sorell were lucky if they could go through Hell's Gate the same day. Often there was more delay. All ships had to wait for the flag at the signal staff to go up. This was the sign that the bar was passable. Once a ship was inside the bar, the long journey was over.[5]

The first survey of Macquarie Harbour was made in January 1819 by Lieutenant Phillip King. Subsequent attempts, in March 1820 by the Surveyor-General of New South Wales, John Oxley, to enter in the *Governor Macquarie* were unsuccessful. When the convict settlement was established on Sarah Island in January 1822, the region was not only unmapped but also unexplored. Subsequently, many of the convicts who were incarcerated there believed that just over the hills to the north "lay China".

An Island of Incarceration: A contemporary view of Hell's Gates, the entrance to Macquarie Harbour; looking north across the tidal race of the entrance to the entrance lighthouse from a site near the old convict signal station on Cape Sorrel. To the left (west) is the vast Southern Ocean and to the north is Ocean Beach which was, and remains, a feared lee shore in the not infrequent periods of heavy winds. Photograph courtesy of Nucolorvue, with acknowledgements.

Lieutenant John Cuthbertson was appointed as Commandant (and Magistrate) of the foundation settlement. Together with three civilians (including the Assistant Surgeon, James Spence) and a garrison detachment of the 48th Regiment of Foot, the party sailed from Hobart in the *Prince Leopold* and the *Sophia*.

Their human cargo consisted of—

- 11 convict artificers and mechanics, to receive indulgence after a period;
- 11 convicts not under secondary transportation, including the pilot's crew,
- 44 "male convicts of incorrigible character";
- 8 female convicts.

As the ships approached *Hell's Gates*, the *Prince Leopold* was unable to negotiate the treacherous entrance and in the inclement weather was driven past her destination. The *Sophia* "defeated the boisterous state of the weather and dropped her anchors at Sarah Island on the 2nd January, 1822".

Initially, the expeditioners were —

> ... put on the small island [Sarah Island] like survivors of a shipwreck, with some provisions, building materials and tools, to commence a penal settlement. Nearly three months passed before the 'Sophia' arrived again from Hobart with more stores and convicts.[6]

Remains of the convict-built penitentiary on Sarah Island Macquarie Harbour, in Tasmania. Limestone was burnt on the Island for the preparation of mortar and the bricks were locally hand-made by the convicts. Photograph, circa 1982.

The female convicts were initially put on Grummett Island for their own segregation and safety. Subsequently, Grummett Island or Small Island as it was called at the time, became a place of further punishment — a form of tertiary transportation for the worst of the worst.

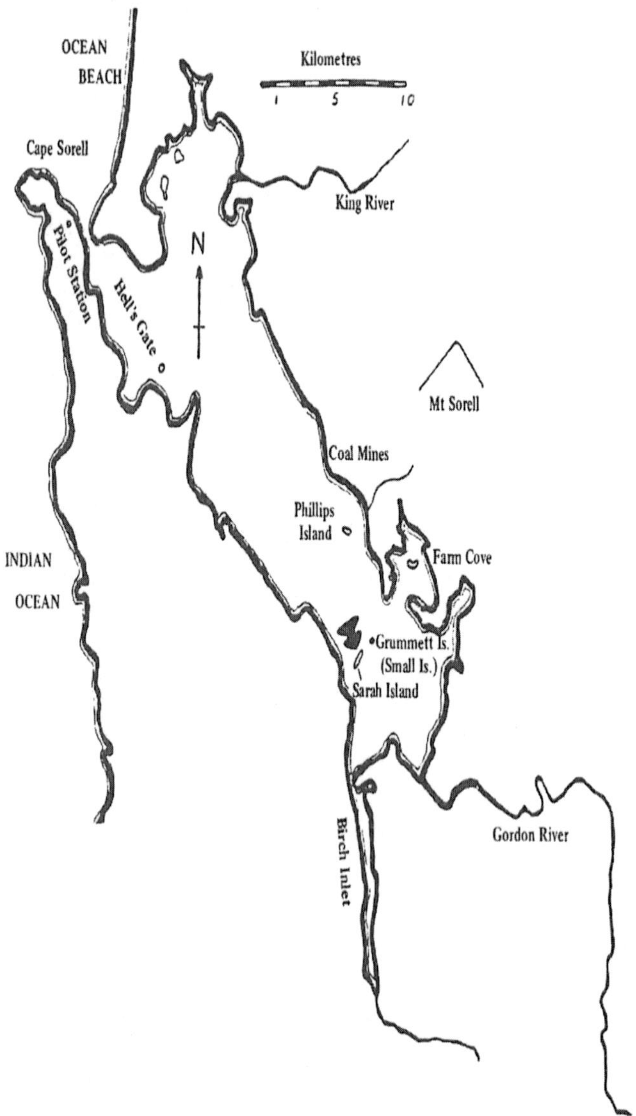

The Macquarie Harbour convict settlement based at Sarah Island (arrowed) on the west coast of Tasmania.

THE GARRISON

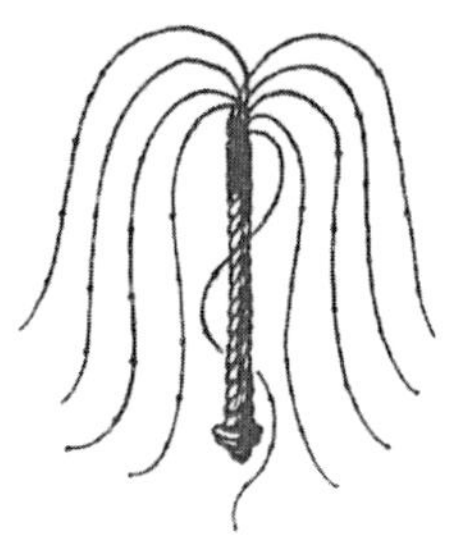

The isolation, the remoteness, the wet-cold and the degradation of prisoners at Macquarie Harbour generated a milieu which made for conditions of the great hardship, not only for the convicts who served their terms of imprisonment there, but also for those garrison soldiers (and their families) and the resident surgeon. One of the non-recidivist convicts had as his official occupation the title of “Flagellator”. The Flagellator and the Surgeon alternated in damaging and then repairing the backs of recidivist convicts.

All the garrison staff longed for the day of their return to Hobart, usually after a minimum of twelve months' service. Notice of their posting back to the relative civilization of Hobart or Sydney came in the supply ships, usually the *Sophia* or the *Prince Leopold*. A flagstaff on the hill at Cape Sorell was manned by a tiny military detachment; and signalled the arrival of one of the ships hopefully bearing orders for a soldier's or surgeon's recall. T.J. Lempriere, who visited Sarah Island in 1832, wrote that —

> ... the signal staff was twenty-one miles from the settlement. It was amusing to see with what eagerness the officers used to strain their eyes in attempting to see the always-wished-for signal. Indeed, we were so often on a short allowance of some part of our rations, besides the anxiety naturally felt to hear from absent friends, or the

> news from headquarters, that the announcement of the signal flag being up always caused a great deal of excitement amongst every class of the free inhabitants, and we may add, of the prisoners, for each man perhaps hoped that his own name might appear amongst those ordered for removal to Hobart Town.[7]

Macquarie Harbour was occupied as a prison during two distinct periods. The first of these, from 1822 to 1833, was the infamous period when the penal settlement was used primarily for punishment of recidivist prisoners and a supposed deterrence for those who might be contemplating further crimes. It was occupied on a second occasion for a period of twelve months during 1846 and 1847. In this period a second attempt was made to exploit further the natural resources of the region, particularly the stands of Huon pine which grew about its shores and along the banks of the Gordon River which drained into the Harbour.

Throughout the second period only trusted convicts were sent to the Harbour.[5,8]

Islands of Incarceration: View of Sarah Island from the south, looking north-east, showing (at left) the slipways of the convict shipyards. Here were built more than ninety ships and boats, including the 225 tonne barque, '*William IV*', over the eleven year period (1822 – 1833) that this industry operated. The signalling flagstaff (right) is at the northern tip of the Island. No convicts ever escaped from this island of incarceration. From a water-colour by W. B. Gould, courtesy of the Mitchell Library, Sydney, with acknowledgements.

THE SURGEONS

A posting to Macquarie Harbour was a hardship post for the surgeon stationed there. Those surgeons who were deployed were not high on the promotional ladder, either in the Colonial Service or within the Medical Department of the Army Office. Paradoxically, the need for those special medical skills of a confident personality, a good diagnostician, one experienced in treatment and preventive skills — such become the greater under these circumstances of great exigency. Such is always the case — the more remote and isolated, the more difficult the medical work; and thus too are the required medical skills and experience the greater.

In all, eight doctors lived on Sarah Island in the eleven years of its First Convict Period. One of these, Dr Charles Henry Theodore Constantini, was there as a convict following his transportation for recidivist burglary in 1833. Another, Dr Walter Williams, was appointed as Surgeon on the 5th August, 1829, but was captured by his convict patients, en route to Macquarie Harbour. He was aboard the ill-fated *Cyprus*, the supply brig bringing urgent food and provisions for the population of 400 men and women at the short-rationed convict outpost. Whilst the *Cyprus* was in Recherche Bay on 15th August, 1829, some of the thirty-one convicts overpowered the guard whilst the Officer-in-Charge, Lieutenant Carew, was temporarily nearby in a dinghy, fishing. The mutinous convicts locked the soldiers in their cabin below decks, fastened the hatches and poured boiling water on them through the hatchway. Further threats of pouring boiling pitch, brought surrender. The captain, the soldiers, the surgeon and the women and children were landed at five different points along the beaches of Recherche Bay along with some non-mutinous convicts. The *Cyprus* had been provisioned for four hundred men for six months, and the convicts sailed her to China.

The six surgeons who served at Macquarie Harbour stayed at Sarah Island for an average twelve-month posting. They were a disparate group. Only one, Dr William Dermer, was university qualified. He had obtained his Doctorate of Medicine degree from the University of Edinburgh in 1825, after the successful submission of his thesis, "De Synocho". At least two of the surgeons, Robert Garrett and William Dermer, were accompanied by their wives and families during their time of service on Sarah Island. The Tasmanian Archives contain several letters from Mrs Garrett, wife of the Second Assistant Surgeon Robert Garrett. She wrote several times from Sarah Island to the Colonial Secretary, pointing out that her husband had been appointed (on the 29th October, 1829) to Macquarie Harbour for twelve months on Station; and that by 1831 they were still there and that she "needs make a formal request for the transfer of her family from Macquarie Harbour".[9]

The posting of doctors to penal settlements was sometimes a low level punishment for recalcitrant doctors. Others, single men such as Waiter Scott who was the medical pioneer at Moreton Bay[9] and Emile Deplanche who served in the French outpost on New Caledonia for almost a decade,[10] volunteered for such service for enigmatic reasons. Other surgeons had hobbies of botany and zoology and according to the Tasmanian historian, Peter Macfie —

> ... some were doctors who came [to the outpost penal settlements] to shoot and stuff ducks, or to

collect seaweed and send specimens in bottles to each other.[11]

One of the surgeons on Sarah Island was there as a recidivist convict and not as a doctor. He was the burglar, Dr Charles Constantini, also known as John Constantine. Born in Paris, and after graduation as a doctor convicted of burglary at the Old Bailey, he was transported to Sydney where he was assigned as a servant to a Mr Hawkins at Bathurst, circa 1822. In 1825 he was granted the last free pardon awarded by Governor Brisbane on the application of the Captain (Hyacinth Bougainville) of the ship *Valparaiso* sailing for France and England. Constantini abused this trust and robbed the Captain; and was promptly sent back for another seven year term of penal servitude, this time at Macquarie Harbour in 1833. He was a talented, naive painter, later specialising in *trompe d 'oeil* oil paintings of great skill. Mr George Brown, the Tasmanian historian, notes that there is a bank note depicted in one of Constantini's surviving paintings which is so exact a copy that one could almost cash it!

The diseases and injuries of the convicts at Macquarie Harbour were aggravated by the cold, the wind, and constant exposure to water and damp and to the brutality of flogging. Surgeon John Barnes, in a letter to Governor Arthur of the 17th April, 1827 wrote —

> At Macquarie Harbour there is rheumatism, scurvy, dysentery and local inflammations. It is

cold and wet and frequently [there are] sudden changes of weather.[12]

THE CONVICTS

The convicts were the *raison d 'etre* for Macquarie Harbour. Although most were regarded by the authorities as the worst specimens of humanity, some convicts were sent to Sarah Island because they possessed special skills. Masons and carpenters, shipwrights and even the specialist flagellator were needed to ensure that the Settlement could function as a working outpost. Shipbuilding, timber-getting and milling were the principal occupations. Work gangs of convicts would row, sometimes more than twenty-five kilometres, to a timber camp on the shores of the Harbour or up-stream along the Gordon River; after the day's work they would have to row "home", sometimes after dark, to their cells on Sarah Island.

The working conditions of the convicts were extremely arduous and deliberately made so. The men often worked in the freezing water of the Harbour, making rafts of the Huon logs which they cut and transported from the Gordon River and the shores of the Harbour. Cold and freezing conditions with constant skin maceration caused an inordinate number of

skin and chest diseases. Twenty-seven men drowned during the period of the convict settlement. These conditions were part of the “salutary dread” of punishment for recidivists transported to Macquarie Harbour.[13]

One of the inescapable duties of the surgeon was to witness the daily floggings and to administer aid to the victim. Referred to in Official Reports as Punitas or Contusio or Flagellatio, this meant extensive lacerations involving not only the skin and soft tissues, but some destruction of muscle tissue as well. The cat-a-nine-tails at Macquarie Harbour was a unique and more sadistic “instrument of correction” than that used at other penal stations. Dr John Bames, the second surgeon to serve at Macquarie Harbour (from 1823) reporting to the Select Committee on Transportation in London in 1838, gave evidence —

> The annual average number of lashes at Sarah Island was 6744 [for a convict population between 100 and 370]. The lash was a much heavier instrument, and larger ... it was a formidable instrument indeed ...[14]

Every prisoner at Macquarie Harbour dreamed of escape. The problem was the impenetrable rain forest with its spongy, mossy and water-logged floor. Around the Gordon River shores, as tourists today know, visibility is less than ten metres. The forest simply swallowed the escapees up; and on one occasion in March 1822, the pursuing soldiers also, never to be seen again. There was food, but none that the Europeans knew to eat; there were no landmarks and no shelter from the wet and the cold. Yet, always, across the hills lay China.

Islands of Incarceration: Boat building was one of the principal industries at the penal settlement of Macquarie Harbour. A total of ninety ships and boats were constructed over the 11 year period of the First Convict Settlement on Sarah Island. Huon pine, which grew abundantly in the temperate rain forests of the Harbour and of the Gordon River which flowed into it, is one of the most water resistant woods known. This convict-built clinker boat survives at Port Arthur today. Photograph, 1993, courtesy of Professor Gael Phillips, with acknowledgements.

Attempted escapes were common — more than 140 — from Macquarie Harbour, but few were successful! There is no record of any successful escape from Sarah Island itself. Most escapees simply disappeared and were never heard of again. Their bones undoubtedly lie in the primaeval wilderness today. Many would-be escapees returned voluntarily after several days, knowing they would at least survive on Sarah Island. Accepting the inevitable one hundred lashes and solitary confinement seemed a small price to pay. One infamous escapee, Alexander Pierce, ate his fellow escapee, Thomas Cox. The *Hobart Town Gazette* of Friday 23rd July, 1824, reported —

> Executions. On Monday, Alexander Pierce, for murder. ... Picrce's body was, after it had been suspended the usual time, delivered at the Hospital for dissection ...

History showed that the original surveyor of the Hell's Gates entrance, Deputy Surveyor-General G.W. Evans, was correct when he predicted in 1822 that —

> At Macquarie Harbour is the certainty that the convicts sent there can have no communication with the eastern side of the island [Tasmania] for so completely shut in is this harbour by the surrounding rugged, closely wooded, and altogether impenetrable country, that escape by land is next to impossible.[14]

The convict industries at the Macquarie Harbour settlement were shipbuilding, a tannery, farming, an open-cut coal mine, charcoal-burning, lime making, timber-getting, a sawmill, a brick works, a blacksmith's enterprise and a leather-working factory to make shoes.

Isolation and Beauty: The trunk of a thousand year old Huon pine on the banks of the Gordon River, south-west Tasmania. Timber-getting of these trees was a principal industry for the convicts incarcerated on Sarah Island from which they rowed twenty or more kilometres daily to cut this timber. In 1822, the Governor of Van Diemen's Land William Sorell, established the penal colony on Sarah Island to satisfy an "urgent want ... of a local spot of farther punishment, to which the worst Class of Convicts Could be sent, and where their labour would be productive": Photograph, 1993, courtesy of Mr Reginald Graham, with acknowledgements.

Islands of Incarceration: Sarah and Grummett Islands in Macquarie Harbour were places of final incarceration for Governor Arthur's worst or "seventh class" of felon. There is no record of any successful escape from either of these two prison islands. The Cordon River (shown here) flows into Macquarie Harbour. Both the river and harbour were surrounded by impenetrable forests of Huon pine, tree-ferns and the luxuriant foliage of a perpetually wet, temperate rain forest. Convict boat crews rowed from Sarah Island across the Harbour and up the Cordon River to cut Huon pine at these sites. The photograph shows St John's Falls on the Cordon River, Tasmania. Photograph by kind permission of Nucolorvue, of Devonport Tasmania, with acknowledgements.

The indigenous Huon pine, first discovered in 1804 in the vicinity of the Huon estuary, was available in great numbers on the banks of the Gordon River which flowed into Macquarie Harbour. The up to "20 metre long trees were cut into logs and then rolled into the river where they were chained together to form rafts. Convict boat crews then towed the rafts, consisting of about a hundred logs, to Sarah Island. This was an easy job during the summer months when the river could be navigated without difficulties. But during the months of winter and spring, when the river was often in flood after long and heavy rainfall, it could be a dangerous undertaking. Sometimes the chains gave away and the logs chose their own way of travelling down the river. Such accidents always gave a lot of trouble, and it rarely happened that all the drifting logs were recovered."

When the rafts reached Sarah Island convicts had to plunge in the water to seize the logs which often had a circumference of 4 to 5 metres and weighed over ten tonnes. This was the most hated job at the settlement, for the convicted men had to wade waist and neck deep in the cold water, and were in danger of being crushed to death by the massive logs. The logs were piled in stacks up to ten metres high.[6]

The main occupation on Sarah Island itself centred about two convict shipyards, an ambitious and sophisticated enterprise built on reclaimed land at the south-eastern extent of the Island. In all a total of eighteen ships, twenty launches and fifty or so smaller boats were built on Sarah Island including four brigs of some 130 tonnes each, and the barque, the *William IV,* of 225 tonnes. The last boat, the 120 ton brig, *Frederick*, was completed by a trusted group of ten convict shipwrights in December 1833, after the convict settlement had been closed. When the boat finally weighed anchor at Wellington's Head, just inside *Hell's Gates*, to sail for Hobart in January 1824, the convicts overpowered the master shipwright and the soldiers; and sailed the brig to Chile. Three men subsequently drowned and four were recaptured and escaped the gallows to be sent to Norfolk Island. Three reached freedom, probably in America. This chapter closed the story of the First Convict Settlement (1822 – 1833) at Macquarie Harbour.

ABORIGINAL PEOPLES

The treatment of the Tasmanian Aboriginal Peoples is notorious in Australian colonial history. It is to the depths of the colonial record that one descends to learn that the last surviving Aboriginal Peoples of the south-west of Van Diemen's Land were also taken to their incarceration on Sarah Island.

In April 1830, Mr George Augustus Robinson arrived to establish his base at Sarah Island "to effect an amicable intercourse with the Aboriginal tribes of this island [*i.e.* Van Diemen's Land]".

Many Aboriginal women (including Truganini) and their children and some men thus lived in the Penitentiary buildings and the Hospital between 1830 and 1833. Susceptible to European diseases, eleven died in the midwinter of 1833 (including the tribal Chief) and were buried on Sarah Island. The survivors were then further incarcerated on Grummett (Small) Island as a quarantine measure. The survivors, in the final infamy, were transported to Flinders Island — their final island of incarceration — when the Macquarie Harbour penal settlement was closed in 1833.

ENDPIECE

The advantages of Macquarie Harbour as a place of incarceration turned out to be spurious. For every advantage it transpired that there was a greater, indeed often insuperable, disadvantage —

> "the severity of conditions that rendered Macquarie Harbour a dreaded place of punishment had the added effect of breeding discontent and poor morale among the military guard and the civil officers. The isolated low locale that helped to keep Macquarie Harbour so secure also resulted in problems of provisioning and communication by sea ... the bar across the entrance to the Harbour posed problems to shipping links. Although only 180 miles from Hobart, vessels might take weeks to reach Macquarie Harbour and sometimes even had to go around Bass Strait. The soil was barren and the settlement was not self-sufficient in provisions. With the supply ships often delayed by strong seas, the settlement [at Macquarie Harbour] was frequently short of provisions and the convicts prone to scurvy. It was also too small for expansion — as Governor Arthur was to lament, there "was invariably a much larger number of Candidates [for Macquarie Harbour] of the very worst description than were places available".[7]

Any experiment of this nature — to concentrate the most wicked and recalcitrant villains on a tiny island in a remote and threatening environment — was a dangerous one. So it turned out to be in the case of Sarah Island. The first Commandant was drowned whilst attempting to retrieve his drifting supply boat. The terrified Corporal who found himself in charge then “instantly proclaimed military law and flogged all the prisoners”.

This set the pattern of the ensuing years of the settlement until its final closure in 1833. Morale of the soldiers and the surgeon and their families was doomed to be low in a place where the second Commandant decreed that discipline and punishment would ensure “that the convicts may absolutely dread the very idea of being sent there”.

In spite of this official policy, the surgeon Barnes reported that he “never knew a convict benefited by flagellation as they always became more desperate characters than before”. Thus it has always been. Degradation and violence, as the experiment of Sarah Island showed, have no place in any system of reform and rehabilitation.

Wilderness: The convicts of Sarah Island at the Macquarie Harbour penal settlement, on the west coast of Van Diemen's Land cut and milled the Huon pine which grew along the banks of the Gordon River which flowed into Macquarie Harbour. This primaeval wilderness, now preserved for posterity, was impenetrable to escaping prisoners as it is to the tourist visitor of today. The convicts who worked here believed that "beyond the hills lay China". With the author (front left) is Mr Reg Graham, of Macquarie Harbour. Photograph, midsummer, 1993.

An Island Reclaimed: A late twentieth-century view of one of the convict ruins remaining on Sarah Island. The bush has gradually reclaimed the rocky higher ground of this once most-feared of all the British convict settlements. Photograph by the author, February 1993.

Norfolk Island

John Duke

aptain James Cook, RN, during his second voyage to the Pacific, discovered Norfolk Island on the morning of 10 October 1774, at latitude 29° south and longitude 168° east. The Island was used for a penal colony during two subsequent periods — the first from 1788 to 1814 and the second from 1825 to 1855.

FIRST SETTLEMENT 1788 TO 1814

The first settlement on Norfolk Island was established under Lieutenant Gidley King on 6 March 1788. King arrived in the Supply with a party of 22 other persons, 7 free men and 15 convicts. The medical staff consisted of Thomas Jamison, previously First Assistant Surgeon on the Sirius, and John Turnpenny Altree, Surgeon's Assistant. Prior to the establishment of the settlement a landing party with Mr Callam, the surgeon

of the Supply, went ashore to explore. Mr Callam was separated from the party and became the first European known to sleep on Norfolk Island.[1]

The first settlement was intended to prevent occupation by "foreign powers", to utilise the flax and to secure pine timber for the making of masts and yards. It was also used to establish a penal settlement and was to supply food for the infant settlement of Port Jackson.

With the help of Surgeon Bowes, Lieutenant King chose the first convicts on the basis of their characters and their skills. The female convicts came by choice and were offered the prospect of family life. Male convicts were not hardened criminals; and principally had been transported for stealing. Governor Phillip instructed King that suitable couples would be allowed to marry and that the marriage ceremony could be performed by the surgeon, Thomas Jamison.[2]

Punishments at the Norfolk Island convict settlement were less severe and less frequent than those inflicted at Port Jackson. As Valda Rigg suggests, convict life had a 'tolerable degree of comfort' during this first settlement as compared to the second settlement".[3]

This was to play a large part in the health of the convicts. Work was hard. There were provisions for only six months and establishing good crops was essential. Work combined from daylight until sunset with breaks at half past seven for one hour and at half past eleven for two and a half hours. During the hot summer months the convicts were allowed three and a half hours respite in the middle of the day. Their staple foods were Indian corn, fish, cabbage, bananas, poultry and pork. Climate and pests caused crop failures from time to time and food was short following the wreck of the Sirius. However by 1792 wheat, maize, potatoes, cabbages, bananas, pears, peaches, apples, oranges, strawberries, guavas, lemons and limes were flourishing in Norfolk's fertile soil.[4]

Although convict life was reasonable, the men were still subject to psychological humiliation as well as the degradation of corporal punishment. It was the surgeon's duty to attend the sick and to examine the new arrivals. He was in attendance at floggings and to see that the offender was fit to take the punishment; and to order cessation if it endangered life. Twenty-five up to 50 or 100 lashes were commonly inflicted. Under later Commandants, 200 or even up to 500 were ordered on some occasions. Although the lash was the usual form of punishment there were other forms also detrimental to health. Food rations could be reduced or work increased; and this could be accompanied by the wearing of iron collars or leg irons.

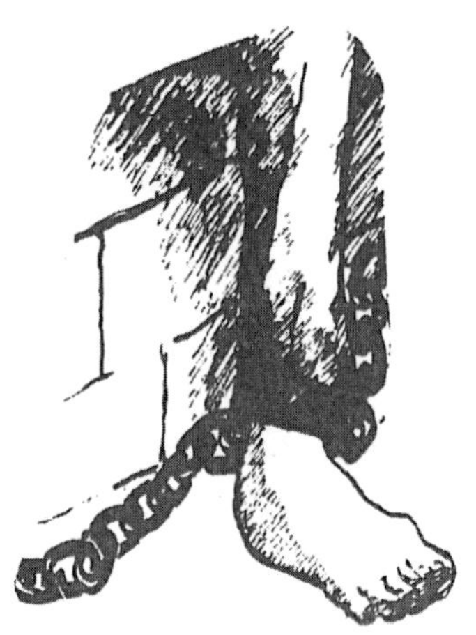

At first personnel were housed in tents but within three months (by late June 1788) all inhabitants were in weatherboard huts with thatched roofs. Later, more permanent residences were built for the surgeons. A hospital was built during 1791 under Lieutenant-Governor Ross.[5] A prefabricated, framed and weatherboard women's hospital of 50 feet by 14 feet, with a height of 7 feet, was built in 1795 at Sydney (Norfolk Island) at a cost of 63 pounds.[6] In 1792 a surgeon received an annual salary of £182/10/0, surgeon's mate £91/5/0, and assistant mate £50/0/0.[7] Nurses were selected from the convicts and received no reward other than their maintenance.[8]

The settlement of Norfolk Island at Kingston during the Second Settlement. It includes the civil hospital (arrowed). From a lithograph entitled 'The Settlement, Norfolk Island' by E. Burgess. Etching courtesy of the Mitchell Library, State Library of New South Wales, with acknowledgements.

In March 1790, the medical staff was increased with the arrival of Dennis Considen who was to be acting assistant surgeon. He arrived on the Sirius on its last voyage. Considen was a pioneer of pharmaceutical research and wrote his Doctorate of Medicine thesis (on tetanus) at the University of Edinburgh in 1804.[9]

D'Arcy Wentworth arrived in 1790.[10] He was appointed as the surgeon on Norfolk Island. Later, he was also appointed as superintendent in charge of the convicts at Queenbrough.[11]

Dysentery was a common illness in the settlement. Frequent "lameness" is recorded in Phillip Gidley King's Journal of 1787-1790. In January 1790 there was an outbreak of diarrhoea which cleared quickly. The surgeon attributed this to —

> ... the Vast quantity's of vegetables that are eaten.[12]

An account of Births and Deaths on Norfolk Island from November 12th, 1791, to October 18th, 1796, gives a further understanding of the diseases which were encountered in medical practice in this settlement.

Death Statistics: 1 month to 2 years, 38 dead —
2 — 18 years, 2 dead —
18 — 30 years, 36 dead —
30 — 45 years, 30 dead —
45 — 65 years, 31 dead.

> Causes of Death: Teething 23 —
> dysentery 45 — cholera morbis 1 —
> obstipation 1 —
> fevers 7 — consumption 8 —
> debility 22 — ives venerea 5 —
> dropsy 3 — putrid sore throat —
> convulsions & epilepsy 4 —
> surfeit 2 — scalded 1 —
> abscess & canker 2 —
> eruptions, scald head,
> mortifications 3
> iliac passion 1 — shot 1 —
> casualties 2 — executed 1 —
> suicide 2 — locked jaw 2.[13]

The nutritional status of the convicts was generally good. Debility was mentioned concerning some convicts and was usually ascribed to improper treatment on the voyage out from England.

> A convict, who was quite debilitated, fell and to all appearances was dead, but by the Surgeons successful Exertions in applying the Apparatus furnished by the Humane Society he was restored to Life but his debility was so great, ... all appearance owing to improper treatment on the voyage, ... that he died a few days after.[14]

The nature of the apparatus mentioned are obscure!

Some convicts devoured their week's ration at one meal. In one such instance on 26th July 1792,

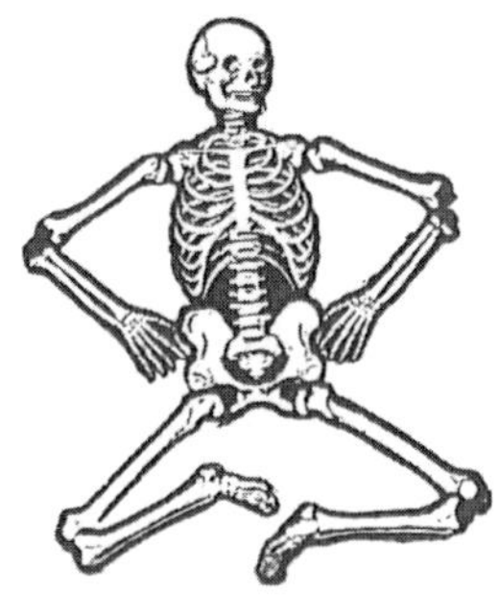

"a convict died at Queensboro ... after suffering inexpressible torments for three days. Not withstanding the Exertions of the Surgeon he died in great agony". His death was attributed to "an indigestion or obstruction in his stomach".

Another convict nearly shared the same fate as the one already mentioned, and from a similar cause. Many continued to devour their week's ration at one meal and the Deputy Commissary was directed to make two servings a week to such.[15] The Commandant, King —

> ... ordered a great part of the fish which were caught, to be given to the surgeon who caused a large Mess to be made of them with Rice, a potable soup and vegetables ...

and similarly with pork. This was a great relief for those recently arrived who "are in general so weak and emaciated that they are little better than invalids". The average number of sick in August 1792 was 91 among whom "extreme weakness seems to be the prevailing complaint".[16]

Dr William Balmain arrived at Norfolk Island on the 4th November 1791 with Phillip Gidley King who had been appointed to serve a second term as Commandant.[17] Balmain relieved Dennis Considen and was also appointed to be one of the two magistrates in May 1793.[18]

Norfolk Island: An exterior view of the ruins of the civil hospital. Photograph, courtesy of Mary Duke, with acknowledgements.

The surgeon reported that between November 1792 and September 1794 there had been 6 civil, no military and 102 convict births; and 1 military, 16 convict and 14 child deaths.[19]

Medical staff varied from time to time. By March 1794 there were listed on Norfolk Island one principal surgeon, two assistant surgeons (civil), one surgeon and one surgeon's mate (military).[20]

However on the 16th October 1795 Balmain wrote to Governor Hunter stating that —

> ... one assistant surgeon is stationed at Norfolk Island and [there is] no person with him capable of taking his charge, in the case of accident or ill-health.[21]

The shortage of medical staff is again mentioned in 1798.[22]

Thomas Jamison arrived in March 1788. He was to serve on Norfolk Island with intermittent absences, until 9 August 1802 when he returned in the Harrington to Sydney to take up the position of Surgeon General.

In May 1805 he wrote to Governor King requesting six additional Assistant Surgeons to meet the needs of the various Settlements formed in the colony of New South Wales, including that at Norfolk Island. He also advised that —

> ... a Judicious selection and nomination should always be made of Surgeons appointed to these Settlements whose local seclusion render the benefits of Medical consultation unattainable; in such a charge as the above it must reasonably follow that those only should be entrusted whose intimate acquaintance with Physical application and competent experience in the Symptoms and progress of Disease shall enable them to act on their own unassisted decision with safety to their patients.[23]

Surgeon Jamison also brought to King's attention that —

> ... important considerations in the economy are tenderness, care, and punctuality in the Nurses and others immediately attendant on the patients; on the exactness of these people in administering at the hour prescribed the Medicines prepared, depend the

success of the Surgeons, but as it is only in my power to chuse [sic] such persons, without any means of inducement to excite their care and attention, it requires an unremitting Vigilance in the surgeons even to exact a partial discharge of duty from these people; therefore [I] beg merely to hint the propriety of allowing a small established gratuity to an Overseer of the hospital, and two Matrons, those persons to be always selected from the Wardsmen and the Nurses whose merits should be most conspicusous.[24]

Norfolk Island: An interior view of the ruins of the civil hospital. Photograph, courtesy of Mary Duke, with acknowledgements.

In regard to the patients' food, Surgeon Jamison recommended that it "be purchased and issued daily by a Purveyor, or let it be contracted for, at a certain allowance for furnishing the Patients with Fresh Meat and Bread at so much per diem, the other necessaries to be furnished by the Crown".[25]

Jamison was replaced as the surgeon to the Colony by William Redfern. Redfern had been transported to Australia on the *Minorca* acting as assistant to the surgeon. He arrived at Port Jackson on the 14th December, 1801. After a short time in Sydney he was appointed Assistant Surgeon at Norfolk Island. His work and character soon attracted the attention of the Lieutenant Governor, Colonel Foveaux, Commandant on Norfolk Island. It was reported that Surgeon Redfern's conduct "merited perfect approbation".[26]

On 19th June, 1803 Redfern was granted a certificate of emancipation.[27] In 1804 Gidley King sent "some vaccine matter" which had been used successfully in Sydney, to Lieutenant-Governor Foveaux. The surgeon was instructed "to make a trial of it among the children at Norfolk". It did not succeed on this occasion. Later the children of Lieutenant Davis (New South Wales Corps) were inoculated at Sydney prior to their departure to Norfolk Island.

"The children arrived with it here when the matter was in its highest perfection, from which it has been communicated pretty well all over the Island the vaccine matter sent by the Principal Surgeon having as usual failed." John Piper, Commandant, reported

"The cow pox has been propagated ... without a single instance of any bad effect".[28]

William Redfern returned to Sydney in 1808; and shortly thereafter he was examined by Dr Thomas Jamison, principal surgeon and Dr Harris and Dr Bohan (surgeon and assistant surgeon of the New South Wales Corps). He satisfied these gentlemen of his knowledge and was given a medical certificate dated September, 1808, the first medical diploma granted in Australia.[29]

John Connellan, an Irishman, was appointed to Norfolk Island in February 1806 as acting assistant surgeon at an annual salary of £182.10.0.[30] No other surgeons were registered in April 1810.[31]

"All persons of the civil department, prisoners, and others employed by the Government" including those at Norfolk Island were admitted to hospital without charge and food was supplied from the Government Stock. This meant that they had —

> ... and other necessaries that the surgeon required and the stores can afford.[32]

Withdrawal from the Norfolk Island Settlement began with the departure of forty-one people in August 1804. Continued evacuation occurred over the following years and the withdrawal was finally completed in February 1814, bringing the First Settlement to a close.[33]

SECOND SETTLEMENT 1825 TO 1855

In June 1824 moves were made to reopen the penal settlement at Norfolk Island. The authorities decided that it would become a prison for the worst offenders. The Secretary of State made it clear to Governor Darling that "no hopes of any mitigation of their Sentences by a removal from thence, should be held out to them".[34] "In England from 1815, with the end of the Napoleonic wars, crime again had become a domestic political issue and 'deterrent' became the watchword of the legislators and seekers of society's revenge".[35]

The first party arrived in the cutter *Mermaid* and the brig *Brutus* under Captain Turton on 6th June 1825, with 57 convicts. All women were withdrawn in 1826 and the prohibition of women was only somewhat relaxed in special cases in the years ahead. There were never any female convicts during the Second Settlement. Using the walls still standing from the first settlement and other available material, temporary buildings were erected. Convicts were required to clear and break up soil from 7 a.m. until 4.30 p.m. with no time allowed for breakfast or dinner.[36] "The 'home', and consisted of 1 lb. flour, 1 lb. salt beef or 10 oz. salt pork, 1 oz. sugar, 1 oz. salt, oz. soap. All [the rations were] issued raw, the men having to cook it as best they could."[37]

There was little improvement over the years and in 1844 Mortlock wrote —

> ... our fare was excessively meagre; at breakfast and supper we ate insipid hominy (made of unsifted Indian corn flour, boiled into the consistency of baked rice pudding, which it resembles only in appearance), nominally sweetened with an ounce of sugar per diem — really, with about half that quantity. A morsel of salt junk, very like old saddle, was served out for dinner, and nauseous, coarse, maize bread, tasting as if it were composed of sawdust. Fresh meat and wheaten flour could be seen only at the Hospital and Commissariat Stores ... the debility brought on by this diet caused many deaths.[38]

Reclamation and reformation of the convicts was not to be the aim on Norfolk Island. Their physical and psychological health suffered from hard work, isolation, poor diet, overcrowding, the humiliation of wearing coarse shabby clothing, ridiculous haircuts and harsh punishment through flogging and imprisonment chained to the floor.[39] There was gross cruelty under some Commandants.

The convict population grew and the sleeping quarters became overcrowded as were facilities for eating and exercising. According to Stuart's report to the Comptroller-General of Hobart Town in 1846 "this gaol is generally overcrowded, is badly ventilated, low, and damp; the prisoners have each a thick straw mat, and a blanket which forms a bed on the stone floor".[40]

Convict Mutiny: A convict headstone in the Norfolk Island Cemetery. Photograph, courtesy of Mary Duke, with acknowledgements.

The Surgeon's quarters, a timber building, "was constructed on the site of the first and second Government Houses dating from the first settlement". The Quarters "contained two apartments, one either side of a central passage. Each apartment contained a living room and two bedrooms". Dr Rott (Surgeon) lived in the east apartment.[41]

> The Civil Hospital was originally built upon First Settlement remains ... The hospital building was marked on the site of the present ruin in

1829 ... it was described as an 'old building, thatched, [for the] Hospital Wardsmen and sick'. It contained two apartments, ... a medical press, two tables, a dead box, in 1832 the old hospital was renovated. The roof was shingled and additions were made in the form of a kitchen, dead house and privy."

Twelve months later the building "consisted of a central section [which incorporated the old structure], four sick rooms, and one exempt room, and two wings. The dispensary was housed in the east wing, the kitchen in the west. The yard thus formed was enclosed on the northern side by a stone wall". The hospital continued to be too small and "numerous recommendations were made for either a new hospital or additional accommodation". At other times plans were laid for a new hospital but these never eventuated. "In the late 1830s a verandah was added on the south side of the courtyard." The hospital continued to be inadequate because of overcrowding and dampness which damaged "the medicines and instruments", and "excessive stench from the privy".

The final work on the building was the addition of one room against the outside of the north wall of the yard. It was constructed in the 1850s. The building was described in 1855 as containing '10 rooms, privy, store, 23 window openings, sashes, doors etc; 1 copper, surgery fitted up with shelves, draws, [sic] press etc'.[42]

In addition to being present at floggings, surgeons were required to supervise prisoners sentenced to gaol in heavy irons, the duration of which was up to two years.[43]

Health of the convicts was generally poor. Dysentery was endemic and this, combined with debility, caused many deaths. Ophthalmia and rheumatic complaints were common. Mortlock reports that, whilst acting as Dispenser or Surgeon's Mate at Longridge, even common medicine was regarded as too good for convicts. Salt water did duty for Epsom salts and dysentery was treated with a decoction made from the bark of a tree.[44]

The convicts sought to avoid their "hard, incessant, irksome and eternal work"[45] through malingering. Sometimes "the internal use of poisonous matter" was practised to produce sickness, in many cases causing death. The self-infliction of dangerous wounds and ulcers through the use of poisonous herbs or severe cuts from a hoe were other means of avoiding work — "intentional burning, scalds, dysentery and the tampering with the eyes to produce blindness were in common practice". This led to over-crowding of the hospital with excess patients. Up to 80-100 were locked up in a room 16 feet long and 12 feet wide.[46]

At times suspected malingerers were threatened with punishment which sometimes led to the flogging of genuinely sick cases. During the time of Major Anderson (1834 – 1839), Dr Harnett reported to the Commandant that a convict, William Castleton, who claimed to be suffering from dysentery, was malingering. He was sentenced to 50 lashes. Dr Harnett attended and intervened after the victim had received 37 lashes. Castleton was admitted to hospital and died 4 days later. He was reported as 'an industrious and strong man'.[47] This was not an isolated case and many were lashed for attending the hospital. Dr Harnett had replaced Dr Gamack whom Major Anderson found refractory. Anderson stated that in spite of "all entreaties, remonstrances, and even threats ... surgeon Gamack remained immovable to his wishes". Dr Harnett was much more subservient and quickly reduced those on the easy list from 100 to 50 and he warned "that if any of them came to him with pretences of sickness, inability to labour, he would be punished".[48]

Major Bunbury sought to deal with malingerers by seeking permission to introduce a modified diet for those who did not work. This was permitted provided that the surgeon's approval was sought first.[49] False pretences of ill-health were used as part of the plan in the outbreak on the 15th January 1834. A group of convicts under the pretext of ill-health were taken to the lock-up to await examination by the surgeon. From there they broke out, overpowered and confined the hospital attendants and some of the patients. The mutiny was unsuccessful.[50] The Rev. Dr Ullathorne, who ministered to the men involved in the outbreak, relates that the men were chained in putrid cells filled with yellow air. When some were reprieved they wept with grief, whilst those condemned thanked God.[51]

With the arrival of Captain Maconochie as Commandant at Norfolk Island in 1840 there was a marked change in the management of the penal settlement. Maconochie was a reformer and he aimed not only to punish wrongdoers but also to restore the convicts' self-respect. He introduced the Marks System in which convicts could earn marks for good behaviour. These marks —

> ... could either purchase extra food or the deduction of so many days from the sentence.[52]

He removed many of the humiliating practices under which convicts had to live and provided suitable buildings for worship and a proper school.

The annual return of diseases treated at the civil hospitals dated April 1841 recorded a variety of diseases —

Catarrhs	15	Debilitas	24
Diarrhoea	20	Paralysis	5
Cholera	11	Vertigo	5
Dysentery	54	Rheumatisms	10
Asthma	7	Morbis Cordis	5
Pleuritis	7	Contusio	13
Pneumonia	13	Vulnics	9
Ophthalmia	40	Mania	10
Felsis	70	Syphilis	5
Epilepsia	10	Uulcus	24

Plus one case of abcessus, asci ties, phsuitis, phthisis, pulmon, sinulat 10.

> Two cases of ambuntio, concussio, tumores. Three cases of anascara, cyannadie gastritis, obstipatio. Four cases of hernia, humoralis, lepra. Total 901.[53]

Administration was particularly harsh and cruel under John Price. With this began a period of terror with inhuman practices and outright tortures. In 1847 the list of prisoners confined to the old gaol gives an idea of the trivial nature of the offences for which they were punished. One convict, Doherty, was charged for speaking to a patient in hospital. James Herewith and J. Fitzgerald charged with malingering, came in from the field to see the medical officer.

One had a very sore throat and the other a bowel complaint. The doctor would not see them because they had not gone to see Fletcher, a prisoner who acted as a medical dispenser, in the morning before they went to work. The men reported that they did not know in the morning that they would be taken so ill in the course of the day.

John Richards, suffering from violent palpitations of the heart, missed muster and was sentenced to "four days' solitary". Jos Colsal was convicted for going to the medical officer without having been first examined by Fletcher, the convict medical dispenser.[54]

Sometimes the constables entered the wards at unreasonable hours with great noise searching for tobacco, dragging men out of their hammocks and pulling their blankets about.[55]

In 1853 the recommendation was made to close down the penal settlement, and by May 1855 almost all convicts still under sentence were moved to Port Arthur. With the arrival of the Pitcairn Islanders in June 1856 the last convicts left for Hobart; and what became the third settlement of Norfolk Island began.

Norfolk Island: Medical equipment excavated from the civil hospital site. Photograph, courtesy of Mary Duke, with acknowledgements.

Islands of Incarceration: The Isle of the Dead (left) with Point Puer (middle distance, right) at Port Arthur, Tasmania. On the Isle of the Dead, less than half a hectare in extent, are buried 1769 convicts from the Port Arthur settlement during the period 1831 to 1877. Point Puer, a peninsula extending into Port Arthur, was established in the mid-1830s as a prison for teenage youths. Photograph, February 1993, courtesy of Professor Gael Phillips.

Melville Island

Convict outpost and the first Colonial Settlement in northern Australia

Brian Reid

he surviving, mainly official, records of the colonial establishment of Fort Dundas on Melville Island (1824 – 1829) demonstrate well the paradox of the conflicting attitudes towards the convicts in much of early nineteenth century Australia. On the one hand the skills of the convict 'mechanics' were prized and they were distributed with considerable care. On the other hand their status as felons was constantly evoked with erosion of their productivity a frequent result.

Melville Island was the first colonial establishment in northern Australia. It also demonstrates clearly an alien perception of the tropical environment by both troops and convicts. There was much more reluctance to live off the land than in temperate settlements and this had serious consequences, particularly for the convicts.

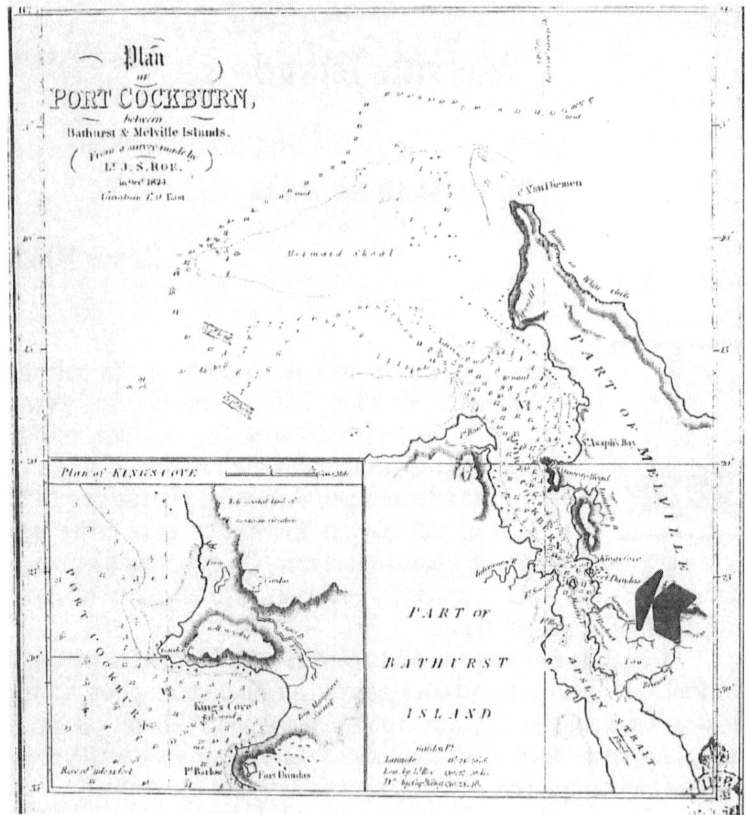

Convict Island and Colonial Outpost: The original hydrographic survey map of 1824, off the coast of the present-day Northern Territory of Australia, north of the City of Darwin. It shows the two islands — Bathurst Island (lower left) and the north-western extent of Melville Island. Port Cockburn separates the two. Fort Dundas (arrowed) was the site of the first colonial outpost to be established in northern Australia. Captain James Bremer RN, with a military garrison of the Third Regiment of Foot, and a party of 44 convicts built Fort Dundas after their arrival in September 1824. Map courtesy of The Mitchell Library, State Library of New South Wales, with acknowledgements.

THE ARRIVAL IN 1824

In October 1824 Captain James Bremer RN of HM Warship Tamar and the supply ships *Countess of Harcourt* and *Lady Nelson* made their way as instructed to Aspley Strait, the narrow divide separating Bathurst and Melville Islands. They had been at sea for about six weeks sailing from Sydney up the east coast before the south east 'monsoon'. The expedition sailed south through the difficult shoals and currents to a small bay on the Melville Island side of the strait which Bremer subsequently named King's Cove. There they anchored and despatched an exploring party to the forest fringed tidal mud flats of the cove in search of the fresh water that would make settlement in the vicinity possible.

Bremer's instructions were to form an 'establishment' not a 'penal settlement' as was for example being considered at about the same time for King George's Sound.[2] Bremer was therefore seeking a site that was defendable, where he could visibly take possession according to the conventions of the day and from which he could provide 'protection' to commercial shipping and trade.[3] A fresh water stream was found at the southern end of the Cove and as the dry season was well advanced the find was considered significant. Just beyond the stream was a moderately elevated flat topped point protected from the waters of the strait by a shallow rocky escarpment and of sufficient proportions to accommodate a fort and supporting buildings. Bremer named the site Point Barlow and he decided to proceed with the construction of what was to become Fort Dundas.

The decision of the Colonial Office to proceed with an establishment also required the New South Wales Governor to make available sufficient 'mechanics' for the task.

This was a considerable strain on the resources of the free' mechanics. An advertisement was lodged in the Sydney New South Wales Government and an initial attempt was made to recruit 'Gazette' with the following conditions applying to successful applicants

> ... passages and provisions [will be] found them by the Government and [they] will be allowed Rations for six months after their arrival provided for half of that period they devote their services to the Crown.[4]

The mechanics would be able to charge for their services after that time and perhaps apply for a grant of land. Three free mechanics were recruited; Henry Feathers, William Potter (nail maker and blacksmith) and Edward Chapman (sawyer).

It was necessary for Governor Brisbane to make up the required workforce numbers and skills from his convict pool. Yet, as Captain Bremer observed, this measure occasioned some difficulty.

> As Melville Island was outside his jurisdiction Sir Thomas Brisbane had no power to detach convicts for labour at the proposed settlement. But the difficulty was obviated by obtaining volunteers from the convicts.[5]

The convicts, for their part, were led to expect an offer of a 'Ticket-of-Leave' on the completion of twelve months satisfactory service. In addition to the three free mechanics, forty four convict labourers were included in the establishment party. They comprised a wide variety of skills; sawyers, plasterers, blacksmiths, stonemasons, nailers, quarrymen, brick makers, coopers, shoemakers and general labourers. The settlement party as a whole comprised about one hundred and ten people. Most of the remainder consisted of a detachment of the Third Regiment of Foot and a supernumerary corps of Marines. Captain Bremer expressed his concern to the Governor's office that when compared to the forty four convicts the troops at his disposal 'would only amount to forty nine firelocks'.[6]

The Commandant and his convict labour force promptly set to work to construct the fort. A square wooden palisade six feet in height with a surrounding ten foot deep trench was quickly erected. On the western side three gun emplacements were built facing the strait. A stone and timber low tide jetty was laid at the foot of the paint with a wood and thatch

Commissariat storehouse nearby. Accommodation for officers was constructed within the fort. In accordance with his instructions Captain Bremer then handed over command to Captain Barlow of the Third Regiment and on the 12 November 1824 set sail for India in HMS *Tamar*.

The convicts and troops constructed wooden huts or, as Bremer referred to them, 'good and comfortable cottages', outside but close to the fort. This was despite the general conviction that the 'natives are understood to be of a ferocious disposition'.[8] A well was dug near the cottages and their occupants were encouraged to prepare gardens.

THE WET SEASON 1824 TO 1825

The establishment party set sail from Sydney with twelve months supply of food and comforts. This was intended to provide for the forthcoming wet season, allow time for the preparation of gardens and enable the colony to survive until regular supplies from the islands to the north could be obtained. The Colonial Brig Lady Nelson was promptly despatched to the islands. So too was the privately owned merchant schooner Stedcombe soon after it arrived.

The main food items available to the settlement from the Commissariat store were flour, biscuit, preserved meat, suet, raisins, salt pork or beef, peas, oatmeal, rice and sugar. The Navy Board Regulations were used as a guide to quantities. Tea, soap and spirits were also available. Fresh meat, usually fish, was substituted for salt meat when plentiful. An allowance of spirits was available to the military.

Melville Island: A contemporary "View of Fort Dundas, taken from Garden Point" — from P. P. King's 'Survey of the Intertropical Coasts of Australia'. Built in 1824, the convict outpost of Fort Dundas on Melville Island off present-day Darwin, was an island of incarceration for skilled convicts from September 1824 until its abandonment in August 1829. Courtesy of the Mitchell Library, State Library of New South Wales, with acknowledgements.

The Commissariat managed the supplies with some independence although ultimately subject to the Commandant. The parsimonious tradition of the Commissariat was soon evident when fish substitution was a possibility. The clerk wrote in November 1824 that 'fish have been caught in great plenty and the prisoners have since received them in lieu of meat rations'.[9] At the same time Captain Bremer wrote 'our supply of [fish] is very precarious and we sometimes have been a week without taking sufficient for everybody'.[10]

The Naval concept of a 'ration' was extended to the prisoners by the Colonial administration qualitative and quantitative changes to reflect their status. This principle was made clear to Major Lockyer at the penal settlement of King George's Sound in 1826. He was advised a 'common ration' would be issued to the prisoners according to a provided scale. He wrote —

> ... The Government has a right to their labour, and no extra meals will be allowed as a means of stimulating their exertions.

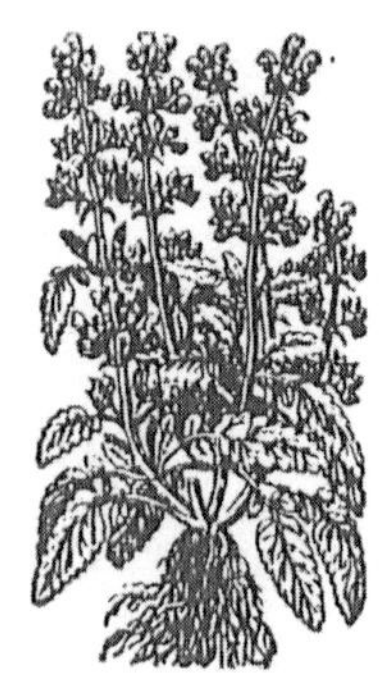

Tea, sugar and tobacco were 'indulgences only and not to be issued in the event of misconduct'.[11]

It is unlikely that raisins or preserved meat were part of the standard ration for convicts for within a few weeks of arrival at Melville Island many became ill with bruising, bleeding gums, painful swollen joints and fatigue. Severe scurvy afflicted many of the convicts throughout the next few months of the wet season. Charles Turner, the settlement medical officer, recorded the grim details in his 'Return of The Sick', November 1824 – April 1825.[12] Of the forty-five prisoners, four died from scurvy and twenty-three others were formally taken off work duties because of scurvy and placed on the sick list. The Commandant, Captain Barlow —

> ... having so few prisoners in health during the rainy season ... [was] obliged to employ some of the soldiers ... giving them the usual military allowance.[12]

The situation was further aggravated by the failure to obtain suitable supplies from the islands to the north. The Stedcombe disappeared on her first voyage and was feared taken by pirates. The Lady Nelson returned empty handed twice and also disappeared on her third voyage. A similar fate was thought likely.

Nor did those in the settlement believe help was available in the hinterland. Those at King George's Sound at much the same time, scoured the local area for what they termed wild celery. In the alien environment of Melville Island the hinterland was believed to hold no such bounty. All exploration was carried out by armed parties following the violent altercation with the Island's Aboriginals within a few days of landing.

The rations-based divisions within the community were plainly revealed by the remainder of Dr Turner's 'Return of the Sick'. Of the thirty-two men of the detachment of Royal Marines, two were placed on the sick list from 'scorbutus'. Of the twenty-one men of the Third Regiment (Buffs) there were also only two placed on the sick list from scurvy.

All of those in authority acknowledged that lime juice and fresh vegetables were required to terminate the outbreak but supplies of these, for general distribution, were soon exhausted. Not withstanding this there were different interpretations of the susceptibility of the convicts to scurvy. Major Barlow believed that scurvy 'came in with the north west monsoon'. Major Campbell, Barlow's successor, was of the view it was 'an endemic disease arising from some peculiar local cause'.[14] Dr Turner thought 'privation' arising from 'exhaustion of labour in a tropical climate and exposure to damp during the rainy season'[14] was an important contributing cause. The convict view of the matter was not officially recorded.

The severity of the scourge prompted Dr Turner to make representations to the Commandant to alter the 'Rations' issued to the convicts. Pre-served meat was issued regularly and 'farinaceous food' was substituted for a proportion of the salt meat. An unprecedented daily allowance of spirits was made available to all prisoners. A 'good weatherboard hospital containing sixteen beds' was completed in March 1825.

THE DRY SEASON 1825

The measures already taken, together with a slow increase in produce from the gardens, led to considerable improvement in the health of the convicts at Melville Island. By the time the south-east monsoon and the dry season were well entrenched there were only a few on the sick list. Dr Turner remained concerned about 'three or four inveterate cases of scurvy I expect no favourable termination to'. In August 1825 the first relief ship from Sydney arrived. Provisions were replenished and Captain Barlow was able to report that the 'prisoners ward in the hospital was unoccupied'. Captain Barlow was also able to report his satisfaction with the behaviour of most of the prisoners and of his intention of giving them Tickets of Leave the following month. He wrote

> I think they will accept the terms given to the free men, by which means I shall have the benefit of their labour for the rest of the year and before it expires I am in great hope of hearing from you of their future destination.[15]

Captain Barlow was seeking in particular, clarification of his authority to grant land to prisoners with Tickets of Leave.

THE WET SEASON 1825 TO 1826

The settlement's second wet season commenced in late 1825 with widespread fears of a return of scurvy. It did not occur on a significant scale and in February 1826 Captain Barlow was able to report 'the people of the settlement are in good health'. In February 1826 the Sir Philip Dundas arrived from Sydney with a relief detachment of the Fifty Seventh Regiment. It also arrived with instructions to Captain Barlow to 'use his own discretion on the question of land grants'.[17]

The Sir Philip Dundas brought an additional sixteen convict workmen. Once again a significant range of skills was represented; sawyers, plasterer, blacksmith, stonemason, nailer, quarry-man, boilermaker, cooper and shoemaker.

A prisoner named Richardson, from the Botanical Gardens in Sydney, and his wife were also included in the new arrivals. He was to take charge of the seeds and plants, for which he was to receive an annual salary of 25 pounds.

The arrival of the new group of convicts accentuated the problems of the Ticket-of-Leave men. Captain Barlow issued twenty-seven 'Tickets', and for each man willing to work beyond the three months and then required to purchase rations, he was prepared to pay two shillings a day. Resentment, however, was growing; the Ticket-of-Leave operated only in the area of the settlement where there was little sign of the trade and commerce that had promised profit and opportunity. Many of the men wished to return to Sydney where there was a good possibility of a further Ticket-of-Leave issue and perhaps higher wages. They also claimed the free passage that had been promised on the completion of twelve months satisfactory service.

THE DRY SEASON 1826

The senior officers had stressed their wish to be relieved. In September 1826 the *Isabella* arrived with the new Commandant, Brevet Major Campbell and the new medical officer, Assistant Surgeon John Gould. Dr Gould was engaged at a salary of a guinea per day. The *Isabella* also brought news of the growing concern of the London based merchants at the failure of the development of trade at Melville Island. An alternate north coast site was being considered. This did little to appease the discontent among the convicts. Four free men and one Ticket-of-Leave man were granted permission to return to Sydney with the *Isabella*.

Major Campbell promptly set about re-establishing order among the prisoners. He issued a set of 'dry weather regulations':

> The working hours for the prisoners will be daylight to 8.00 a.m., 8.30 a.m. to 11.00 a.m. and 3.00 p.m. to sunset. The public work is to be issued on every day except Sunday on which both prisoners and Ticket-of-Leave men are to attend Divine service at 9.00 a.m. in the military barracks. The overseer will see that every prisoner is in his quarters every evening at 8 o'clock.

Major Campbell also sought approval to construct new cottages for the prisoners and Ticket-of-Leave men. The existing ones were located near the swamp and were, contrary to Captain Bremer's earlier description, 'comfortless, small and unwholesome'

THE WET SEASON 1826 TO 1827

The north west monsoon at the end of 1826 brought with it more than rain. In a break in the weather in December fever struck. Five military and one convict died from what was probably malaria.[19]

Most of the settlement was seriously afflicted and little constructive work was possible. In April 1887 a cyclone substantially damaged most of the buildings, the jetty and the gardens. Scurvy would once again prove a problem, particularly for the convicts.

Uncertainty was now added to the resentment of the convicts for Major Campbell had issued instructions that only temporary repairs were to be made whilst he sought advice from the Governor on the future of the settlement.

For some of the convicts Timor loomed as a possible refuge. Samuel Williams (arms repairer) and Thomas Cox (blacksmith) had both completed their sentence and successfully sought permission to work their passage to Timor on the next supply trip.

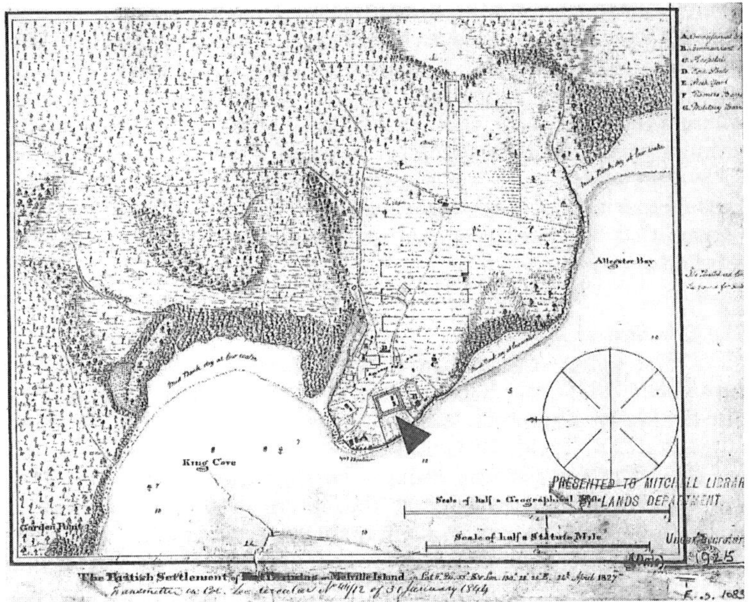

Melville Island — Outpost Convict and Colonial Settlement of 1824 – 1829. Large scale contemporary map of Fort Dundas (arrowed) and surrounds, entitled 'The British Settlement of Fort Dundas on Melville Island April 1827'. This convict outpost, established on Melville Island north of the present day City of Darwin, was the first colonial settlement in northern Australia. Map courtesy of The Archives Office of New South Wales, with acknowledgements.

The Dutch port city of Kupang was frequently visited by foreign vessels and offered the prospect of work. The venture was unsuccessful and within a few months both men were back on Melville Island petitioning for a passage to Sydney.

For others at the settlement, alcohol when available provided some solace. In a scene reminiscent of Sydney a generation earlier, Major Campbell reported in June 1827 —

> ... spirits was introduced and sold among the prisoners by the crew of the Isabella '... in

> partnership with a soldier 100% profit was made ... widespread drunkenness and insubordination[20]

Adding to Major Campbell's concerns with the convicts was an increasing pressure from the second batch of convicts that arrived on the Sir Philip Dundas a year before, for Tickets of Leave and a return passage to Sydney.

THE DRY SEASON 1827

In June 1827 Captain Stirling in HMS *Success* led another settlement party from Sydney to a new site at Raffles Bay on the Cobourg Peninsula some two hundred kilometres to the east. It was hoped this establishment would be of more interest to the Macassan traders. The settlement of Fort Wellington was commenced and Captain Stirling departed leaving Captain Smyth in command. The same sequence of events followed as had occurred at Melville Island and within a few weeks scurvy was widespread.

THE WET SEASON 1827 TO 1828

The 'wet' of late 1827 commenced with fears of illness to compound the resentment and uncertainty of the convicts.

At Fort Wellington scurvy had ravaged the whole community and was made worse by the sudden death of the assistant surgeon, Dr Wood. Captain Smyth sent to Melville Island for help. Captain Campbell set sail for the Cobourg Peninsula and retrieved the worst scurvy cases. He arrived back at Fort Dundas only to find that his own surgeon, Dr Gould, had been fatally speared.

The whole Melville Island settlement was demoralised by these events. Scurvy was very prevalent but contained in its severity by some fresh provisions. The urge to escape again surfaced. Spowage and Faulkener, the settlement's only boat builders, completed their sentences and embarked on board the Anne for Kupang. Clandestine escape was also attempted. As a result of the activities of a prisoner informer, John Francis, Major Campbell detected —

> ... a combination amongst several of the prisoners who had mediated an attempt to escape from the Island and who had already constructed a boat some two miles distant from the settlements.[21]

THE DRY SEASON 1828

In May 1828, Major Campbell, 'having had a complete surfeit of the island', was relieved by Captain Hartley who was also accompanied by a replacement assistant surgeon, Dr Sherwin. Captain Hartley picked up thirteen severe scurvy patients from Fort Wellington on the way. It was at

this time that London made the decision to abandon Melville Island and transfer all its resources to Fort Wellington.

It was to be some months before Sydney and Fort Wellington received notice of closure of the Melville Island settlement, and the despair of the convicts deepened. As Captain Hartley soon reported to the Governor —

> ... a deep rooted discontent of that portion of the prisoners who bear tickets of leave ... sullen, dejected, dissatisfied ... those who have been longest on the island appear to be the most deeply tainted with discontent ... the health of many of those who have been long upon the island affears to have suffered from the effects of the climate.

Whilst Captain Hartley was reaching this conclusion, Dr Sherwin was preparing for him a list of prisoners who were so broken in health that he felt it was imperative they be removed from the island before the next wet season. Yet there continued to be solace. The Amity, now a supply vessel for the settlement, had recently returned from Kupang and in spite of Captain Hartley's 'precautionary measures',

> ... prisoners of the crown found means to land and introduce ... a considerable quantity of gin .. the whole settlement fell into one general scene of riot, tumult and intemperance.[23]

Ultimately the only redress the Ticket-of-Leave prisoners had was to withdraw their labour. In so doing they forfeited their income and their access to the commissariat but, as Captain Hartley observed:

> [the convicts] were indisposed to work ... as they have continued to accumulate [food] to an exertion of mechanical ingenuity in their several callings.

THE WET SEASON 1828 TO 1829

Fort Dundas limped towards yet another wet season. Some of the chronically ill were found a passage back to Sydney. The remainder grimly waited for what they were sure would be instructions to abandon the settlement. Captain Hartley expressed his disappointment to the Governor at the lack of supplies and medicines.

In November 1828 Governor Darling received London's instructions to transfer Fort Dundas to Fort Wellington and despatched the Lucy Anne for that purpose. In December 1828 Governor Darling received further instructions to abandon both settlements. The stores were to be sent to Swan River and the convicts to the penal settlement of King George's Sound.

The evacuation was eventually completed in August 1829.

Major Campbell, writing some years later of the settlement, assessed that of the one hundred and eighty people who resided on the island at some stage when the settlement was active, twenty-six died.[23] Only twenty-two are mentioned in the surviving official correspondence. About one third were convicts and most of those died from scurvy. Malaria and accidents made up most of the remainder. Yet there is more to the balance sheet. The military were generally relieved every year or two; the convicts, even those with Tickets of Leave, were generally only relieved when chronically ill.

The little detail available suggests nutritional disorders were a significant factor. Captain Barker, in charge of the evacuation of Fort Wellington, noted the debilitated state of the prisoners —

> ... the suffering ... is now very perceptible in the men employed in moving and arranging the stores from Melville Island and from the sawyers whose exertions have been great.[25]

The construction and maintenance of the settlement at Melville Island was very much dependent upon the skills of the convict 'mechanics'. Yet much of the death and debilitation that was their reward was a consequence of the prevailing attitudes to Ticket-of-Leave men. This is exemplified by the summary of the inquirer J.T. Bigge in 1820:

... the system of granting tickets of leave to convicts ... too quickly and too abruptly elevates them from a condition of punishment to a condition of comparative enjoyment ... and they speedily loose that sense of humility and contrition which is essential to a state of punishment and reform.[26]

Stradbroke Island

The Convict Era of 1825-1853

Jeanette Covacevich

The Moreton Bay Penal Settlement was established at Redcliffe ... on 14 September 1824, and was moved to a site on the banks of the Brisbane River in May 1825 ... Outstations included a limestone quarry at Ipswich, an agricultural establishment at Eagle Farm, a pilot station at Amity Point, a stores depot at Dunwich, and a military guard at Tweed Heads.[1]

tradbroke Island* forms the eastern boundary of Moreton Bay, and is some 600 km north of Port Jackson Sir Thomas Brisbane, Governor of New South Wales, chose Moreton Bay as a suitable station ...

*The 'Stradbroke Is.' of the convict era in Queensland's history is now two islands — North and South Stradbroke. The narrow sands which once linked these two islands were swept away, following cyclonic weather and flooding in the Logan River, and others nearby in 1896.[1]

(now Sydney), the initial site of European penal settlement in Australia. In the early 1820s,

> For minor offenders ... Moreton Bay would be the fittest depot on account of its distance and almost impossibility of escape, its means of immediately affording employment and subsistence for the prisoners who may be sent there, and the facilities that a penal settlement in the first instance will afford to the free settlers, when it may be deemed expedient to throw open that part of the colony ... [2]

Accordingly, following the advice of John Oxley who had been commissioned to explore the region, Moreton Bay Settlement was established on 14 September, 1824 '... of 50 or so men (thirty convicts, of whom twenty-nine were in irons for the trip [north from Port Jackson in the Amity], several women and children ...'[3]

The settlement was established initially at Red Cliff (now Redcliffe), under Lieutenant Henry Miller.[1-4] Oxley had previously recommended this site as a depot only. He favoured an area on the banks of the Brisbane River, about 20 km away. A site which is now the junction of Eagle and Queen Streets, Brisbane was chosen, and the settlement was transferred there in May, 1825. Red Cliff Point thus had a very short history as a penal settlement.[4]

The convict history of Stradbroke Island is short also. Moreton Bay Settlement/Brisbane ceased to be a penal outpost in 1842.[1] Convicts were not sent to either Amity or Dunwich after 1831.

A Pilot Station was set up at Amity Point, soon after the transfer of the main settlement to Brisbane Town. South Passage, Moreton and Stradbroke Islands, was the entrance to Moreton Bay used by the settlers. It was a narrow passage, made hazardous by a strong tidal rip and sand bars in constant change.[5] This passage and Moreton Bay were surveyed and buoyed first by John Murray Gray, the Port Jackson Pilot, in July, 1825.[1]

Lieutenant Miller had a Pilot (John Tosh), seven convicts and three soldiers based at Amity, by late 1825. Their task was to lead ships through South Passage. Life was hard and hazardous '... The pilot ... with his crew of convicts, used to row through the breakers in the South Passage to meet incoming ships ...'[1] Tosh and two of his former convict crewmen drowned early in 1834. The accident occurred on 13 January, while returning to Amity, after taking the *Mary Elizabeth* through South Passage. The boat overturned on the Amity Point bar.

The Pilot Station operated until 1847, but was not manned by convicts after 1831. Although life at the Pilot Station was hard, the men were not, it seems, totally deprived. An English clergyman, Thomas Aitkins, visited the Amity Pilot Station in 1836, soon after convicts no longer manned the station, *en route* from Norfolk Island to Sydney.

> ... On the beach at the pilot station, I saw three young female natives as naked as they were born. They had attained to a state of puberty, and they were evidently under the protection of the pilot and his staff The reason assigned to their presence was, that the tribe had gone to fight with the natives of an hostile tribe; merely a pretence. The persons of those young females were agreeable and well-formed and their respective ages were from sixteen to twenty years.[1]

The second convict-manned settlement on the island at Dunwich, was established on the recommendation of Governor Darling (in Sydney), 26 September, 1827.

> ... With respect to the Settlement at Moreton Bay, its local situation appears to me highly objectionable. The tediousness and difficulty of the access render it extremely inconvenient.
>
> From the entrance of the Bay to the mount of the Brisbane, on the left Bank of which the Settlement is situated, is about fifteen miles, the intermediate being in general so extremely shoal as to interrupt the Communication.

The Convict Era on Stradbroke Island: The beach at Amity in Moreton Bay, Queensland looking to South Passage. In the early 1820s a Pilot with a crew of convicts from here, would lead ships through the South Passage between Moreton and Stradbroke Islands, en route to the Moreton Bay Settlement. Photo, February 1993, by the author.

The Settlement of Brisbane Town is at least fifteen miles further up the River, so that much time is lost in gaining the Settlement, and small vessels only, of a light draught of water, can accomplish it.

I propose, as a means of remedying in some degree this inconvenience, to form a small Settlement at "Dunwich"* on the Isle of Stradbroke, being the southern boundary of the Bay, for the purpose of receiving in the first instance the supplies sent from this for the Settlement, and the Timber, etc., to be forwarded thence to Sydney.

*Viscount Dunwich was the second title of the Earl of Stradbroke.[1]

According to this arrangement, the Vessels employed in communicating with Moreton Bay will not be detailed longer than may be necessary to discharge and take in their cargoes at Dunwich, it being intended to station a small Vessel at that place for the purpose of conveying the supplies from the Establishment to the Settlement and bringing down the Timber, etc.

The Establishment at Dunwich will consist of a Wharehouse or large store for the security of the supplies ... A few convict labourers will be kept there and a small Guard of Soldiers for the protection of the Establishment. The removal of the Settlement [at Brisbane] altogether might be desirable, but the Establishment at Dunwich will render it, at least, less necessary ...[1]

Several authors[1,6,14] have detailed the establishment of a convict-manned stores depot and military post, and the high (and low) lights of life in the Moreton Bay Settlement. Between its establishment in 1824 and its closure in 1842, Moreton Bay (including Stradbroke outposts at Amity and Dunwich) had eight commandants — Lieutenant Henry Miller (September, 1824 – September, 1825), Captain Peter Bishop (September, 1825 – April, 1827); Captain Patrick Logan

(April, 1827 – October, 1830); Captain James Clunie (October, 1830 – November, 1835); Captain Foster Fyans (November, 1835 – July, 1837); Major Sydney Cotton (July, 1837 – May, 1839); Lieutenant George Gravatt, Lieutenant Owen Gorman (May, 1839 – February, 1842).[1,7,8]

The value of Dunwich, initially named Green Point, had emerged prior to formal recommendations about its use as a stores depot to speed up transfer of cargo between Sydney and the Settlement. A cargo of pine logs from the Settlement had been loaded at Green Point after being held '... in readiness in the Bay for the first vessel which might arrive ...' (Patrick Logan, in *litt*, 25/7 /1827).[6]

Green Point (Dunwich) was a good site because it was close to a water supply, and because the anchorage there was deep and well protected. Logan had strong reservations about the suitability of the site chosen by his predecessors for the main settlement, Brisbane.[6]

This notwithstanding, Dunwich did not develop beyond a loading/stores depot, manned by convicts and their guards, all soldiers. Three incidents stand out in the short penal history of Stradbroke Island — the murder of a convict by the Aborigines (1831), the seizure by convicts of a schooner, *Caledonia*, while she was anchored off Amity (1832), and an affray between the Aborigines and officers and men of the Amity Pilot Station (1832 or 1833). All occurred while Captain Clunie was in charge of the Settlement.

His report (10/4/1831) of the first to the Colonial Secretary for the Colony, Macleay, in Sydney, stated:

> ... this morning one of the prisoners here was murdered by natives in the middle of the garden, at this place.
>
> The only European in the garden at the time, being the unfortunate suffered, I am unable to say even by what tribe this outrage was committed, as a tribe from a considerable distance has lately been in this neighbourhood and I understand have been expressing a determination to be revenged for injuries they state to have suffered from Europeans, upon which subject I can only state, that if such is the case, I am not aware of it, though probably if such a circumstance did occur, it would be carefully concealed from me.[1]

Clunie's report and the accounts of others of the second incident show that eleven men came aboard, very early, from a whale-boat. They put ashore the crew of the Caledonia, save for her Master (Browning), and set a north easterly course to Rotumah in the Fiji Island group, via New Caledonia.

The Convict Era on Stradbroke Island: Dunwich foreshore, Moreton Bay, photographed by the author in June, 1994, from the site where the barracks and store stood in the 1820s and early 1830s, when Dunwich was a depot manned by convicts and their guards.

Browning was rescued by an American vessel. Some of the escapees, died following a quarrel in their ranks. A few attained their precious goal, freedom.

Reports of the third event are conflicting ... 'The affray with the Aborigines at Amity Point has given rise to accounts which differ so wildly that one might be forgiven for thinking that they were unconnected.'[1]

> ... Historical criticism aims at discovering how far a story gives a true account of events as they occurred, and how far it is biassed. If it was written at a later time than the events recorded, the question then becomes: how far has the story been coloured by later prejudices?

It will be of some interest to apply these questions to three accounts of a conflict between the settlers and the

Aborigines on Stradbroke Island in 1833:

1. The Commandant's report to the Government

2. A prisoner's recollections, recorded by J.J. Knight about 1895

3. Aborigines' stories, recorded by Thomas Welsby about 1880.

The conclusions reached concerning prisoners' tales will assist the reader in forming an attitude with which to approach the writings of Knight and of the prisoner William Ross, quoted at some length on subsequent pages.

The affray with the Aborigines at Amity Point has given rise to accounts which differ so wildly that one might be forgiven for thinking that they were unconnected. The connecting link between (1) and (2) is the involvement of Chief Constable Mcintosh, but here they differ in that, according to (1), Mcintosh survived the affray, possibly suffering some injuries, while in (2) he was killed by the natives.

The Commandant's version would appear to be relatively unbiased. Conflict with the natives was frowned upon by the Government, and although the Commandant would have wished to play down the extent to which the natives were injured, he had to be prepared to conduct an official enquiry, should the Governor demand it, so he had to take care to be factual. Of course, it is possible that other incidents connected with the affray were concealed from him by the pilot and soldiers at Amity Point; he allows for any such possibility when he writes "I am not aware that any violence has been offered", in relation to the years prior to the affray.

The prisoner's version bears the marks of a propaganda story; the aim was to depict soldiers and overseers as rogues, civilian officers as fools, and convicts as kind friends of the natives and innocent fellow-sufferers with them. For example, in this version the Chief Constable fails to catch the runaways, whereas the Commandant's version makes it clear that McIntosh was very successful in this regard. In the prisoner's story, the natives tried to spare the lives of the convicts, whereas in the Commandant's version the natives singled out the convicts to be murdered. The prisoner who told the story to Knight probably was unaware of any errors in the facts; he told it as he had received it, and as he had coloured it over many years of retelling.

The conclusion to be drawn from this is that stories told by prisoners should be treated with special caution, if not scepticism. This will apply to the convicts' tales recorded by Knight, the writings of Ross, and also the stories told by convicts to Tom Petrie. The third account of the affray, namely that gleaned from the Aborigines by Welsby, is connected very loosely with the others, yet there is apparently a common origin. The killing of the white man "Chooroong" seems to be reminiscent of the killing of the prisoner twenty yards from the house at Amity Point (Commandant's version) and the killing of the Hut-keeper (prisoner's version). The pitched battle said to have occurred three miles north of Dunwich may possibly be identified with McIntosh's battle with the native (Commandant's version).

The stories of actual events had been added to the natives' repertoire of entertaining legends by the time Welsby heard them. Like the stories of the dreamtime that explained how things began, this story explains how the Aborigines and Europeans were both thwarted in their attempts to win, and so became friends and lived happily ever after.[1]

The Convict Era on Stradbroke Island: This is all that remains easily visible at Dunwich of Stradbroke Island's convict days. The rocks, hand-hewn by prisoners, were used to construct the depot's jetty in 1827. Photograph, by the author, in June 1994.

The Moreton Bay Settlement ceased to be a place for convicts in 1842. Those freed after serving their 'time' often returned to Sydney. They were not replaced, and the convict presence in Moreton Bay Settlement was reduced progressively.

Convicts again figure in Stradbroke's history in 1853. Life on Norfolk Island is well known to have been especially brutal,[9-12] a result probably of its being reserved for 'those convicted of serious crimes, especially for capital respites'.[2] Ten convicts escaped the hell of Norfolk by jumping their guards, while on a work detail to unload the Lord Auckland. They stole one of the ship's boats and 14 days later, landed on Stradbroke at either Adder Rock near Point Lookout, or Amity Point. They threatened a

Philippino fisherman, Fernandez Gonzalez, and stole his stores. This provoked a fracas with the Aborigines at Amity. Freedom was short, and spent making raids for food. They ended their days, in irons again, in Van Diemen's Land.[12]

> Stradbroke‘s beaches and some of its bush are not very different from the way they were when the convict castaway, Thomas Pamphlett and his companions first landed there in 1823, following their escape from the settlement at Newcastle.[13] Pamphlett was to return to Moreton Bay Settlement. In January, 1827 he disembarked there from the Alligator, a prisoner again.[13] (There is no record that he was ever assigned to either of Stradbroke's settlements.)

Stradbroke's shorelines and bars still change daily with the seasons, and also on a longer time scale. The passage between Moreton and Stradbroke is still treacherous. Many ships have come to grief there, since the days when convicts rowed the Pilot to lead ships through the passage. Nothing stands in Amity from Pilot Station days. Dunwich remains a port — for tourists and residents, and for the shipment of sand and fish from the Island. Two structures remain from its convict days. Below the park, the site of the Dunwich convict station storehouse and barracks, are the remains of the station toilet pit, designed to be flushed by high tides.[14]

A wall of rocks, hand hewn by convicts in 1827 to make the Dunwich Depot's jetty, is still visible, now covered by modern fill, concrete and bitumen to expand the town's loading facility. The causeway can be seen best at low tide from the fig-tree shaded park on the northern side of the present ferry loading complex.

Cockatoo Island

An Island of Incarceration in Sydney

Catherine O'Carrigan

It is unlikely that any convict of the penal days was given to fantasising about what he would do on a desert island. In the early decades of the colony of New South Wales some convicts, having been transported over 12,000 miles from their homeland were again subjected to "transportation" to islands within Port Jackson. The first temporary one was Pinchgut Island. It was later transformed into a military post and became Fort Denison in 1857. The second was Goat Island on which iron gangs from 1833 were landed for the building of a powder magazine and a wharf. Less than a mile from Sydney Cove, workers in chains excavated and constructed the military magazine. Once completed, it was considered to be a "powder keg" and one too big a temptation for offenders to be housed there.

The final penal settlement within Sydney Harbour was that of Cockatoo Island. It was the largest of all, about 40 acres in extent. Its average height above sea level was 50 feet. It lay some four miles westward from Sydney Cove, and was surrounded by deep water. Its aboriginal name was Biloela, a reference to the flocks of noisy cockatoos which festooned its red gums.

Geologically, the island was an indurated patch of rock dating from the Triassic Age; and one that had resisted total disintegration during the erosive scooping out of the Harbour valley prior to the latter's later submergence. The fossil remains of a giant salamander-like amphibian, were found on Cockatoo Island in the1880s.[1]

Readers of *The Australian* on January 17 1839 became aware that Governor Gipps had given instructions for a gang of men to be landed on Cockatoo Island to be employed in quarrying stone and cutting flagging, which would be sold to defray the expenses of the establishment. A major decision of the Government was to use the labour of those convicts to excavate from the solid sandstone large grain stores or pits, "in the shape of bottles" twenty feet deep, on the crown of the Island. For many years these were in use as the government grain stores. The rubble was used as a filling for a stone quay, where bagged wheat was unloaded from sailing vessels bringing it from the Hawkesbury and Hunter Rivers and from Van Diemen's Land.[2]

In his Despatch of July 1839 Governor Gipps notified the Home Secretary that prisoners from Norfolk Island had been transferred to Cockatoo Island by means of one of the first colonial Acts brought in after the coronation of Queen Victoria. Men in irons, or men undergoing cumulative sentences, commonly called in the Colony "doubly convicted", were alone allowed to work for the benefit of the Colony, being at the same time fed, clothed and maintained at the expense of Great Britain. Men labouring under simple sentences of transportation, if employed for the benefit of the Colony, were to be fed, lodged and maintained at the expense of the Local Government.[3]

At the time, an excess of wheat production caused a considerable decrease in the market price. It was thus considered advisable to store the grain for future use. In his Despatch of November 30 1840, Gipps reported that the quantity of wheat then stored in the underground granaries or silos was 20,000 bushels, but that additional silos were in progress. If the price of wheat continued to be low, he proposed to increase the Stores to about 100,000 bushels. Each silo was capable of holding from 3000 to 5000 bushels of grain.

Being hermetically sealed, grain of any kind could be preserved for years. The total exclusion of air also entirely destroyed any weevils or other insects that might have been in the grain at the time it was placed in the silos. Wheat from India had been much infected with weevils when put into the silos in December 1839; but there had not been a living insect of any kind when the grain was taken again from the silos in March 1840.[4]

When the British Imperial Convict System ended in New South Wales, arrangements were made to transfer the penitentiary at Norfolk Island to the control of the Government of Van Diemen's Land. The proclamation of Governor Gipps of Cockatoo Island as a gaol was made in June 1841.

Prisoners were then put to work building a strong stone-walled gaol on the Island and also in quarrying stone to be lightered to Sydney Cove as filling for the reclamation of Semi-Circular Quay. In 1842 William Westwood, known as Jackey-Jackey, a convict turned bush-ranger, attempted to escape from Cockatoo Island by swimming, but was captured by the Water Police.

Sydney residents learnt from *The Sydney Morning Herald* of July 16 1842 that with regard to available labour, of the total number of confinees on Cockatoo Island 165 were iron-gang men, 84 were Norfolk Island expirees, and 74 were settlers' men under Colonial sentence. Mention was made of the superior quality of the building stone on the Island. The Island was proclaimed a Prison in 1844 following an Act introduced by Windeyer in the Legislative Council of New South Wales.

Cockatoo Island in Sydney Harbour, showing the cells for the convicts and the signalling flagpole, 1856. From a watercolour by Allan Macpherson, courtesy of the Mitchell Library, State Library of New South Wales, with acknowledgements.

In his Report to the Committee, Governor Gipps defended the bringing of a large number of convicts from Norfolk Island claiming that the operation of the Act had been most salutary. Upon arrival, the men brought from Norfolk Island were placed, not in Hyde Park barracks, but on Cockatoo Island and their conduct had been such as to vindicate the Act fully, and indeed to prove in a remarkable degree the policy no less than the mercy of it.[5]

By the mid-1840s Governor Gipps could see further use for the Island. In his Despatch of November 12 1845 he informed the Home Government of the necessity for Dry Dock accommodation at Sydney. He felt advantages would accrue to the Colony and to the Empire at large. He suggested Cockatoo Island as the best adapted for a naval establishment, not only for a dry-dock, but also for a slip for hauling the ships on the Island. He had directed the labour of the convicts in clearing and preparing the site.[6] The Lords of the Admiralty, however, refused permission for the scheme to continue.

With the change of Governor to FitzRoy, one of the first requests of the new governor was for some remuneration for the Visiting Magistrate, Captain Long Innes, who for five years (since 1842) had fulfilled the role of Magistrate on Cockatoo Island without payment.

Captain Long Innes noted that convicts of the most desperate and abandoned characters had been confined on Cockatoo Island. Some were awaiting removal to an outpost penal settlement whilst under sentence of transportation; others were imprisoned there for safe custody when such were unfit to be entrusted to the ordinary service of the Government. Such was the vigilance exercised by the authorities in charge of the Island that no convict in irons had ever effected his escape, and only one out of irons had done so.

Of the 450 incarcerated there, 145 had been convicts trebly convicted and under sentence of transportation to Van Diemen's Land.

Their constant plots, intrigues and attempts at insurrection had rendered daily visits at dawn quite usual by the Magistrate, Long Innes. FitzRoy requested £100 per annum for the Magistrate. It was approved in January 1848 at a rate of £150 per annum, but was not made retrospective.[7]

With regard to the Dock, which the location of Sydney rendered essential, the Legislative Council of New South Wales had voted £4500 for its construction during the year of 1848.

Laying the foundation stone in the base of the great excavation of the FitzRoy Dry Dock on Cockatoo Island 1854. From the June 17, 1854 Edition (page 109) of 'The Illustrated Sydney News', with acknowledgements.

FitzRoy notified the Home authorities that since the Island was a place set apart for the coercion of convicts under Colonial Sentence, the latter would become disposable in consequence of the discontinuance of transportation from that Colony to Van Diemen's Land. To Earl Grey he proposed the decommissioning of the convict establishment in 1848. Convicts under cumulative sentences were to be placed at the penal establishment on Cockatoo Island. Such prisoners as might be sentenced to punishment were deprived of their Ticket-of-Leave, or were returned from private service. Convicts were also kept

on Cockatoo Island and supported from the Convict Funds during the periods of their sentence, until removed to Norfolk Island.

In 1848 there were eighty prisoners under punishment at Cockatoo Island being men whose original sentences had not expired. On 31 March fifty of these men were transferred to Norfolk Island in the brig Governor Phillip. On the return of the brig, another thirty-one were also transferred. Sixty-six prisoners, under cumulative sentences, remained;

> ... and those, with any future ones sent to the Island would have to be maintained at the expense of the British Treasury.

Provisions and clothing for the one hundred or so prisoners were £558 for the year.[8] From 1848 the Hyde Park barracks ceased to hold prisoners; any remaining being removed to Cockatoo Island. Chaplains were allowed to minister on the Island. On 6 July 1850, the Roman Catholic Bishop Davis wrote to the Colonial Secretary giving his observations regarding accommodation for the men. He was the first to see beyond the limits of a Penal Island and the first to plan for the future of the inmates. He proposed the erection of a building to be used as a Church and School house, and the establishment of a School with a free Schoolmaster.[9]

The silos continued to be a Government asset. H.W. Johnson, in May 1851, applied to purchase 4000 bushels of wheat; and the firm of Thomas Barker and Co. required 6000 bushels for its two windmills above Elizabeth Bay in what is now central Sydney.

In November 1852 there occurred an outbreak of influenza on the Island. The Medical Adviser wrote to the Colonial Secretary about the crowded state of the prisoners there.[10] Ten months later, 28 September 1853, the existence of scarlatina on the Island was reported by Dr G West, newly appointed.[11] The Visiting Magistrate in July 1855 reported that certain invalids and other prisoners were unfit to labour on the work of the Dry Dock.[12]

Although excavation of the solid sandstone had commenced in 1847 on the Dry Dock, it was on June 5 1854 that the first stone of its ashlar lining was laid by Governor FitzRoy, an engraving in a contemporary *Illustrated Sydney News* showing him with the foundation stone of the sill. The Crimean War was raging abroad, and appeals in Sydney were made for the British Regiments' families. When the first vessel HMS *Herald* docked on December 1 1857, the Dock was by no means complete. Charles Cowper, Colonial Secretary under Governor Denison, made plans in late 1857 for a Board of Inquiry into the management of Cockatoo Island. The immediate trigger was the irregularity of boat provision for Chaplains to the Island while the remote cause was the general partiality and injustice of the Superintendent, Charles Ormsby.

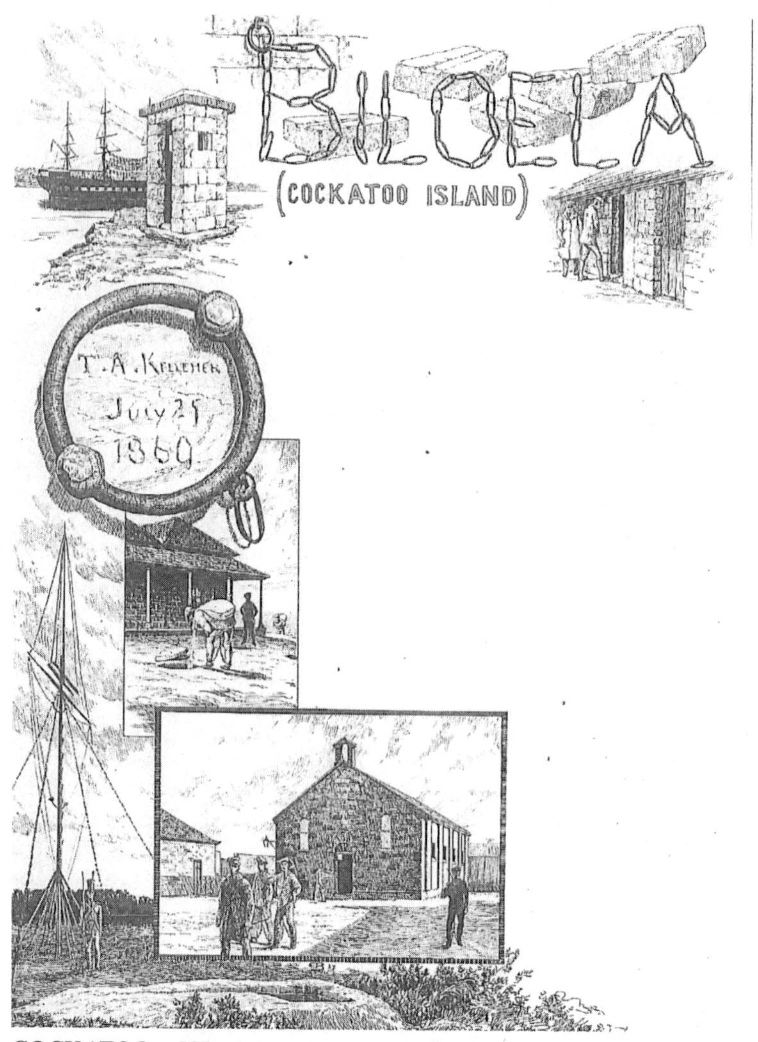

COCKATOO ISLAND IN SYDNEY HARBOUR. A steel-engraved montage of buildings and the well on Biloela, the 'Place of Cockatoos'. Signed 'B.E.' this 1889 reproduction is courtesy of the Dixson Library, State Library of New South Wales, with acknowledgements.

Ormsby had been in the Prison Service for forty-four years, twice at Norfolk Island as Assistant Superintendent of Convicts and also as Visiting

Magistrate. Aged sixty years, he had been for sixteen years in charge of Cockatoo Island indeed since its penal inception. Ormsby took personal privileges, but exacted strict obedience and conformity from prisoners.

The Chairman of the Board of Inquiry was Sir William W. Burton, Judge; and the associates were Captain Ward R.E. and E.C. Merewether, Clerk of Executive Council. Cowper pointed out to the Judge that some of the Island's difficulties arose from endeavours to combine the two objects of making the Island a penal establishment on the one hand; and on the other of employing convicts on executing a great public work.

Henry Parkes was the proprietor of *The Empire* and had run a series of leaders and letters critical of the management of the Island on the second, fifth and ninth of October, 1857. The most damning letter had come earlier on 19 February from John Pendrill, currently a teacher but who formerly had been a Church of England Chaplain at Cockatoo Island for nine months (July 1856 – March 1857). The Catholic Chaplain, Rev. Patrick Kenyan, had been attending the Island for twelve months, seeing to the needs of 150 prisoners, and had made no complaint, even though he had suffered the inconvenience of inadequate transport. It appears that the well-equipped boat, a vessel for conveying Officers and Chaplains to and from the Island was often taken by Ormsby for pleasure trips and picnics accompanied by his friends. Consequently when the Reverend Pendrill came to departure time, he was appalled to see a short boat, lying low in the water, inadequately crewed, which he had to share with the Roman Catholic Chaplain and a convict in double irons. It was a gusty day. The waves splashed over the bow, thoroughly soaking the hapless prisoner and the clerical clothes. Moreover, one rower complained he could not work his oar so deep in the water was the boat. Wet boat journeys of four miles in Sydney Harbour were further injustices suffered by the benighted inhabitants of Cockatoo Island.

Pendrill's assessment of the Superintendent's character was to believe the latter "... to make his arbitrary will and pleasure the only recognised law on Cockatoo Island". He included the observation that the Superintendent had a petty and overbearing spirit; and added that the abuse of unlimited authority which Ormsby had either received in trust or else usurped, created a feeling of general dissatisfaction throughout the Island. The writer summed up some general principles —

> In a penal establishment, where the law vindicates its claim by inflicting its severest penalty, the general administration, even in its minutest details, ought to be conducted in most entire submission to law on the part of its officers, or, in other words, on fixed and definite principles. Even prisoners have certain rights, and when these rights, small though

> they be, are respected, when no petty or extra-judicial inflictions are added to their just judicial sentence, it is felt that justice reigns supreme, and the criminal feels that whatever he suffers he suffers justly.[13]

Pendrill continued by highlighting the offence against justice on the part of the administrator, whose office it was to exact from others the penalties of violated law, himself continually violating the principle of law in little things. One of the illegal sports Ormsby had condoned was that of sparring, permitting two convicts to box in the Prisoners' Yard, with a large number of spectators and a few of the free Officers. He had even permitted his son to be coached. Captain Mann had been eight years Engineer of the Dry Dock, with J.H. Thomas, Civil Engineer, and T. Easton for eight years the Foreman of Works.

SICKNESS AND DEATH ON COCKATOO ISLAND

The Inquiry also revealed grave health concerns on the Island. The Government Medical Officer, G. West, depended on advice from the Visiting Magistrate, Samuel North having succeeded Captain McLerie in 1856. There was always the fear that prisoners who had been on Norfolk Island might commit the crime "that cannot be named", although little evidence surfaced.

Exposure on an isolated part of the island was a punishment for even suspected escape attempts. The sole official in the Hospital was a Dispenser, of whose qualifications no check could be made, as he claimed to have lost them. He had apparently helped once in the Royal Navy. His name was J.F. Peers and he kept a personal journal, now a valuable archive of medical treatment of convicts of the day. He wrote how one young prisoner, Daniel Dunmore, aged 21, had been forced to remain on an exposed area during inclement weather, and autumnal equinoctial gales in Sydney Harbour can be violent.

Admitted with pleuritis to the Infirmary on March 28 1856, the patient complained of great heat, thirst and restlessness. During the night he had a —

> ... violent acute pain on one side, and was unable to lie on it; had difficulty in breathing; flushed countenance; expectoration bloody; tongue coated; the pulse strong.

The next day brought no improvement, but a slight diarrhoea. Two days later the febrile symptoms had abated, but there was great dyspnoea and the tongue was much coated. The patient died the following morning, three days after admission. The Dispenser's notes give a first-hand account of the treatment of pneumonia in Australia of that era —

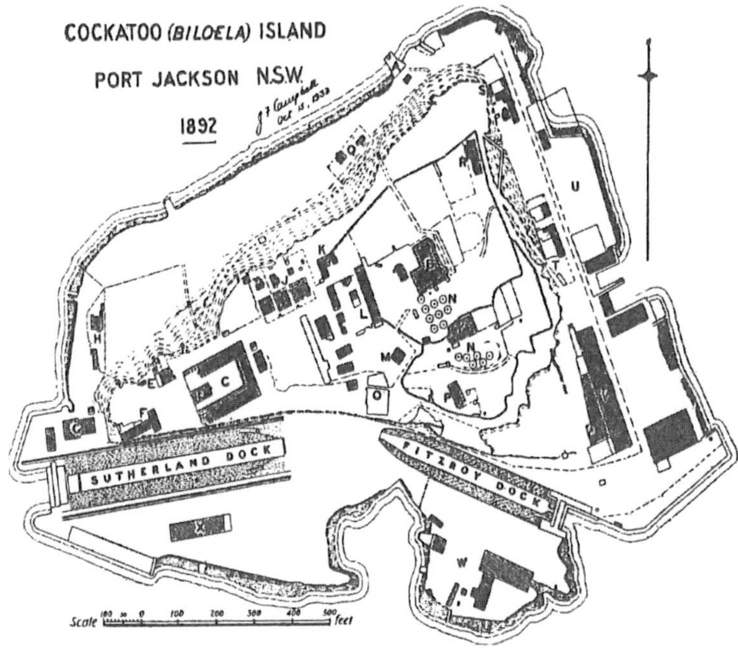

A plan of Cockatoo Island Sydney Harbour, in 1892. Courtesy of FJ Campbell and the Journal of the Royal Australian Historical Society (1932), with acknowledgements.

LEGEND

A "Steamers' Wharf".
B Principal residence .
C Principal dormitory buildings.
D Mess room.
E Governor's resid ence.
F Gaol, store, kitchen, warder's room and garden .
G Engine and boiler buildings, caisson chamber on west.
H Engineers' residence;
I boat-house and ways.
J Warders' residence, dispensary
K Deputy Governor
L Mess shed, laundry and store on east, dormitory and work-room on west.
M Deputy Matron's house.
N Wheat silos excavated in rock, bottle shaped (now sealed).
O Two water tanks excavated in rock.
P and **S**. Cottages.
Q School and appurtenances.
R Dock clerk's house .
T Warders' houses.
U Reformatory recreation ground, open sea-bath on north.
V Blacksmiths' and machine shop, offices, and rock-tank.
W Carpenters' shop, surveyors' store, sawmill, etc.
X Repairing shed and store, wharf on west.
Y Dock master's house, gardens adjoining on east .

TREATMENT

Dec. 28th – Cerat. Ant. Tart. Pulv. Jacobi. gr ill. Venesectio ad. drachms xvii. Foment Caliae. ad.pect Hyd. Chlor. gr.iv statum. Emp. Ly. Hoe.

Dec. 29th – Hyd .Chlor.gr.ii; Popii, gr. p. Ant. Pot. Tart. gr.l/6. 4 horis. G W peacs.

Dec. 30th – Rep. Pulvis. Liq. Amman. Acet. drachms vi; Vin Ipecac minims ii. Recipe Opio. Camp. minims ip. M. Camp. drachms vi. Nd. drachms ip. sexh's horis. Sumeno. Emp. Ly. Hoe.

Dec. 31st – Rep. Mist. 8 o 'cl. Rep. Pulvis. Hyd. Chlor. gr. iii. Ant. Tart. gr.l/6. Pulv. Opii. gr. p.4 horis.

Another patient was the 79 year old convict, William Murphy, who had been transported on the Canada. The Dispenser's private journal records his case, one of bronchitis progressing to pneumonia.[14]

WILLIAM MURPHY, aged 79, "Canada", admitted to its Hospital on Cockatoo Island December 3rd, 1856.

DISEASE, WITH DETAILED SYMPTOMS

Bronchitis

Dec. 3rd –This man who has been perpetually exempt since his arrival on the island and who is very much debilitated and suffering from scrotal hernia, applied to me at l0 p.m. for the first time; he complained of chills and oppression of the chest, with quickened and laborious respiration. I at once admitted him to hospital, applied mustard plasters, and cupped him; and considering his advanced age, and debilitated frame, that there was considerable danger, sent for Dr. West.

Dec. 4th – Dr West attended; approved the treatment pursued and prescribed.

Dec. 5th – Symptoms aggravated; pulse higher; cough, expectoration, and febrile symptoms increased.

Dec. 6th – No improvement. Dr. W. ordered treatment to be continued.

Dec. 7th – Breathing with the greatest difficulty; copious tracheal rattle; all the symptoms of acute suffocative catarrh developed. Death ended his sufferings at 2 p.m.

J.F. PEERS .

Following the Official Inquiry a tightening up of the rules of management followed, with the Chaplain and the Surgeon suggesting that a Visitors' Book be maintained to record dates of attendance. In mid-April 1858 the Visiting Magistrate transmitted the Rules regarding the conveyance of official Visitors for the approval of the Colonial Secretary. On 5 May the Visiting Magistrate recommended that certain prisoners be allowed Task Work credit if they sang in the Choir on Sundays. Was this an echo of Maconochie's "Mark System", the idea of rewards for good conduct? Although the late twentieth century takes such concepts as good conduct remittance and parole for granted, they were novel ideas on Norfolk Island and Cockatoo Island in the nineteenth century. The singing, which provided an emotional release for the inmates was, in all probability, introduced by Father John Therry, who was at Balmain from 1856 onwards, his Church being the nearest to the Island of Cockatoo.

The Visiting Surgeon on 30 April 1859, again a changeable season, spoke of the necessity of flannel clothing being supplied to the convicts. Perhaps the workman's grey flannel sweat shirt stems from that time.[15]

PROBLEMS OF SECURITY; AND THE FEAR OF REBELLION

In the Cockatoo Island Dockyard there was great activity in the late 1850s. The P&O Steamship Benares docked there, announced the Department of Land & Public Works on 25 May 1859. By mid-July Father Therry was reporting the dangerous state of the roadway from the wharf upwards on the Island sandstone being notoriously brittle.

Renewed security came to the Island in 1859, with the Brigade Major in Sydney reporting the Standing Orders of the Officer Commandant in the event of a Military Guard being again placed there. Some months later the Brigade Major reported the want of proper communication between the Military on the Island and the mainland.

The Ordnance for the Dock Establishment was reported as unserviceable by the Department of Land & Public Works on 20 August; while the Magistrate of the Water Police announced the dissolution of the North Shore Ferry Company, and made alternate plans for the conveyance of the Military Guard to the Island.

The Engineer in Chief and Superintendent issued a Draft Code of Regulations for the FitzRoy Dry Dock on 14 September 1859. He also requested the purchase of a daily newspaper.

The close of an eventful year saw the Colony of Queensland gaining secession from its parent New South Wales, and by 12 March 1860 the Military were drafted to Queensland and the Guard withdrawn from Cockatoo Island.

Little human touches creep through the screen of officialdom. A Cockatoo Island name appears in the first *Annual Report of St Vincent's Hospital* in 1858, "... from James Keenan, Police Constable on the Island a £1 donation". This was followed the next year by another donation of a guinea. One of the Island's policemen wrote to Father Therry on 24 August 1860. Peter Grimley wished to visit him on the Sunday, as he had obtained leave of absence and proposed, God willing, to get married on Monday.

The decade of the 1860s brought tensions to the surface, probably because of the continuation of protracted penal conditions, still latent twenty years after Transportation was abolished. There seemed to be little remission from stone-making in the mason 's yard. On March 17, 1860, fifty-eight of the prisoners refused to work on St Patrick's Day, it being a Holy Day in Ireland. So many were the claims that the Chairman of the Convict Classification Board was called to examine the list of convicts claiming Indulgences.

The first two months of the year 1861 revealed feelings of rebellion. In the midst of the hot summer, on January 23, the Engineer in Chief and Superintendent forwarded to the Colonial Secretary a list of the prisoners sentenced to Cells, and that meant being transferred to close confinement in Darlinghurst Gaol. The Visiting Justice received a Statement of the prisoners' grievances. The punishment that had been inflicted on the refractory prisoners was reported, and advice sought from the Magistrate as to the carrying out of the sentence. The Visiting Surgeon of the Darlinghurst Gaol wrote concerning the prisoners sentenced to close confinement. The next day, 24 January, seventy-three prisoners sentenced to Solitary Confinement were transported across the Harbour by boat to Darlinghurst Gaol. The following day the Crown Solicitor at Sydney requested the attendance of certain convicts from Cockatoo Island as witnesses at the Supreme Court. Five days later the Sheriff at Sydney offered suggestions concerning certain prisoners then in Darlinghurst Gaol. He asked for an immediate supply of First Quality Bread for the Cockatoo Island prisoners confined in the Cells. By the 13 February came the expiration of the sentences of the Island men. They had spent three weeks in dark solitude.[16]

Meanwhile, a new medical man, Owen Spencer Evans, applied to be appointed as Surgeon to Cockatoo Island on 30 January 1861.[17] Throughout the sixties, some awareness of the state of health of the prisoners emerges from their request for the Catholic Chaplain. For example, this archive reveals that on 26 February 1867, one William Goodman wrote urgently to the Superintendent that James Clarke, a patient in the Cockatoo Island Hospital, was in a dangerous state and wished for the Priest. Then on 27 April the Superintendent reported that the prisoner Thomas Grimes had dysentery and was dangerously ill, so was requesting the Priest. On 18

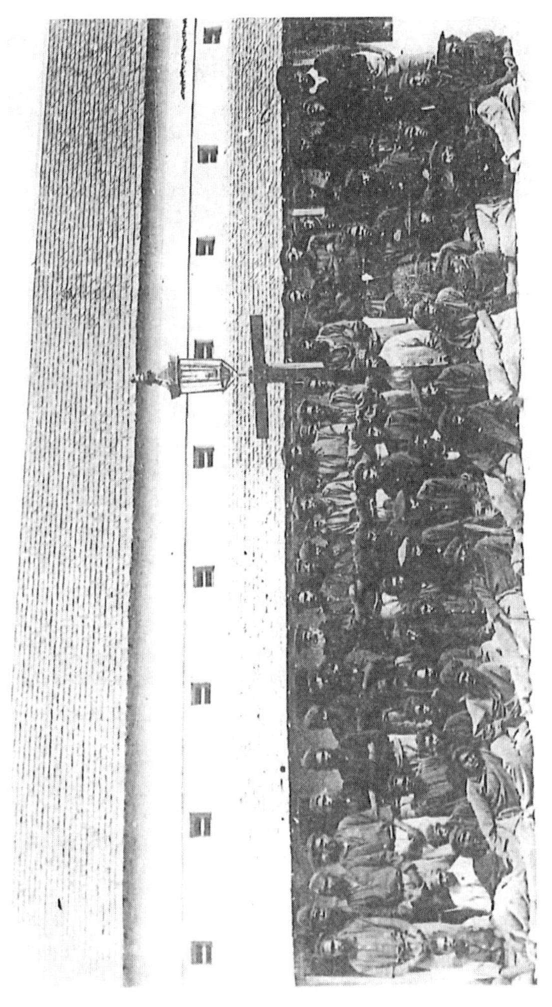

Rottnest Island — An Island of Incarceration: Rottnest Island was established as an Aboriginal Prison in 1838. During its functional life between 1838 and 1902 some 3,400 male prisoners were transported across the eighteen kilometre, shark infested water gap from Fremantle in Western Australia. Of these 314 are known to have died, a death rate of 10 percent. This photograph, circa 1850, is labelled 'Inside the Quadrangle' and shows the regulation prison garb and cap worn by inmates. Photograph, courtesy of The Library Board of Western Australia, with grateful acknowledgements.

March of the following year a petition came from George Lynham, a prisoner suffering from low fever and who was dangerously ill, also asking for the Catholic clergyman.[18]

Because of their acknowledged visitation of prisoners in the Parramatta and Darlinghurst Gaols, the Sisters of Charity from St. Vincent's Hospital were in constant demand especially for preparing the inmates who wished to approach the Sacraments. So an approach was made on behalf of Cockatoo Island by the Chaplain, the Rev. George F. Dillon on 20 June 1866. The reply came the following day from Henry Halloran on behalf of the Colonial Secretary, Henry Parkes, granting permission for them to visit the Roman Catholic prisoners on Sundays.[19] The first Island of Incarceration these nuns had been Norfolk Island for Captain Maconochie in 1841 had written to Governor Gipps suggesting the value of obtaining their help (not pursued); and they had also been requested for Van Diemen's Land to which three Sisters went in 1847.

Although the intention of the Government was to have all the prisoners removed from Cockatoo Island by the end of 1868, it was to take another three years before that evacuation was completed. From Goulburn came a petition on 4 January 1869, signed by the Roman Catholic Rev. P. Dunne and others, in favour of the prisoner James Clune, then serving a sentence on the Island. The reply was positive, with the Government authorities remitting the remainder of the prisoner's sentence. Henry Halloran on behalf of

Colonial Secretary John Robertson informed the Rev. Dr Polding that the Government and Executive —

> ... had been pleased to approve that the Penal Establishment at Cockatoo Island be abolished as soon as arrangements could be made for the removal of the prisoners there from; and that therefore the services of the Rev. John Kelly as Roman Catholic Chaplain would not be required after such removal.

In 1871, the last male convicts were removed from the Island. The former prison buildings, surrounded by a high stone wall on the crown of the Island were put to a new use as a "reformatory" for women prisoners and for female juvenile delinquents. They were to remain there until 1908, even during the noisy excavation in 1884 for a second and larger Dry Dock, the Sutherland. Like so many of Australia's other islands of incarceration, Cockatoo Island today shows but the ghosts of times past. May those who visit think of the fallen who served their sentences there; and work towards better methods of reform today.

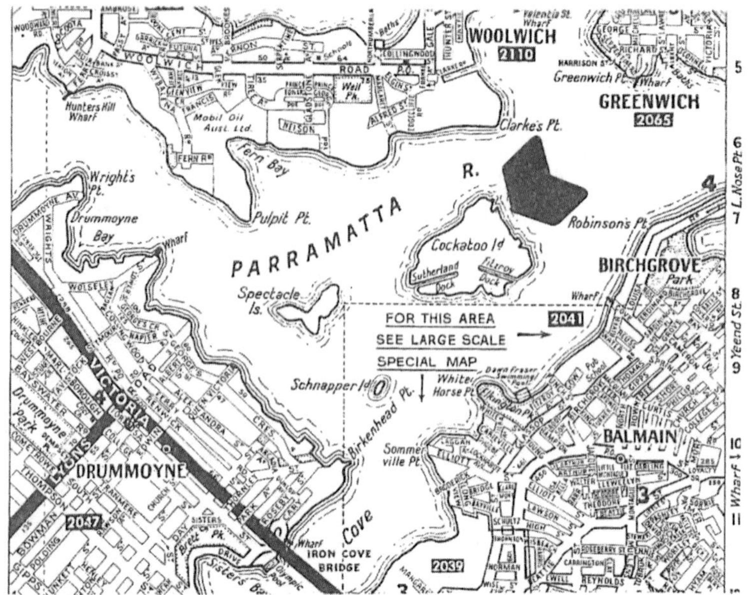

Cockatoo Island in Sydney Harbour, west of the Harbour Bridge. A contemporary street map showing the relationship of the two maritime docks — Fitzroy Dock (built in 1854) and Sutherland Dock (built in 1884). Courtesy of Gregory 's Street Directory, with acknowledgements.

Rottnest Island

A dark history off the West Australian Coast

Peter Burns

Until about 6,500 years ago, when sea levels rose at the end of the last ice age, the coastal outcrop which is now Rottnest Island was part of the mainland of Australia, where Aboriginal Peoples had hunted and fished for many thousands of years.[1] Now eighteen kilometres from the port of Fremantle on the Western Australian coast, the island is shaped like an elongated lozenge, 11 km long and 4.5 km at its widest point, with its greatest height above sea level being 4.5 m at Wadjemup Hill, the Aboriginal name for the island. From the time of its isolation from the mainland Rottnest remained uninhabited until European settlement.

Rottnest Island was discovered accidentally by Dutch seamen seeking a shorter route to the East Indies. One Hendrick Brouwer pioneered an alternative route sailing south from Capetown to 35° south latitude, then due east for 6,000 km before turning north, hopefully missing the dangerous reefs off the Western Australian coast. Many ships went off course and some reached the coast. The first of which we have knowledge was the *Eendracht* captained by Dirk Hartog, who in 1616 landed on the island some 700 km north of Fremantle which now bears his name. He was not impressed by the harsh country that he saw. He left an inscribed pewter plate nailed to a tree, to record his landfall. This plate is now in Fremantle's Maritime Museum. Charts recording details of the coast of Western Australia gradually evolved; and Rottnest Island first appeared on these charts in 1627.

The first Europeans did not land on the Island until 1658. These were the crew of the Waeckende Boey, under Captain Samuel Volkerson, who reported seeing

> 2 seals, 1 wildcat and the excrement of other animals.

A shore party of fourteen was landed, but later a storm blew up and Volkerson was unable to land. After waiting for signs of the party he assumed, wrongly, that they had perished, and he sailed for Batavia. One month later four of the marooned survivors reached Batavia in an open boat. There was an official inquiry into the circumstances, but Volkerson was exonerated from blame.

Willem de Vlamingh was the next to land in 1696, and named the island Rottnest, after the abundance of large 'rats' (now known to be quokkas) which he saw. The French vessel, *Naturaliste*, anchored at Rottnest in 1801, and Joseph Bailey, one of the naturalists aboard, identified the 'rats' as small marsupials which he thought to be a species of kangaroo. These quokkas are unique to Rottnest Island.

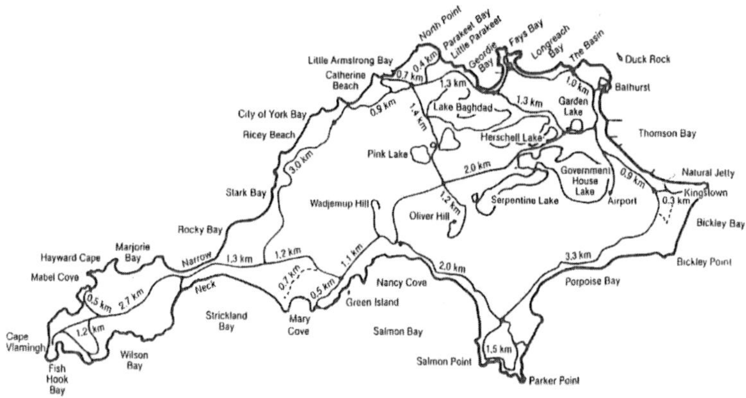

Rottnest Island — An Island of Incarceration: The Island is situated some 18 kilometres from the port of Fremantle, in the Indian Ocean, off the coast of Western Australia. Measuring 11.0 km by 4.5 km at its widest point, its 1900 hectares have been the home to two prisoner populations — that of the Aboriginal Prison 1838 – 1903; and in the twentieth century, a World War I internment camp. This contemporary map of the Island courtesy of The Rottnest Island Authority, with acknowledgements.

During that time of the Napoleonic Wars, the British were concerned that the French presence in these waters could endanger trade with the colonies in the east of Australia. Matthew Flinders was sent from England in 1801 to chart the coast more accurately, a feat accomplished during his circumnavigation of the continent in 1802 — 1803. Phillip Parker King was the next to land in 1822, but he could

find no fresh water and gave a poor report of the Island's potential.[2]

In 1829 the colony of Western Australia, also known as the Swan River Colony was proclaimed.

Rottnest Island: Island of Incarceration — On Rottnest Island off the Western Australian coast from Fremantle, Aboriginal men were incarcerated over the period 1838 – 1903. This sculpture, in the Island Museum of today, records their plight. Photograph, 1994

In the next two years at least twelve settlers requested land grants on Rottnest Island with a view to farm, fish, mine salt from the salt lakes, or simply to escape from the "hostile natives" on the mainland. Robert Thomson, William Clarke and Robert Lyon were three pioneers who did establish themselves on the Island building with the local limestone, and cultivating the sandy soil. There was frequent conflict between the Swan River settlers and local Aboriginal Peoples. Many Aborigines were imprisoned in Perth gaols, hunter-gatherers who were unwilling, not unreasonably, to accept the white man's laws. It was

found that imprisonment in cramped mainland gaols was devastating to their health and morale; as similar lessons have been re-learnt in the late twentieth century. They were totally unused to close confinement.

The proposal to use Rottnest Island as a gaol was thought to provide Aboriginal prisoners with a reasonable degree of freedom, yet one isolated from the mainland by shark infested waters. This did not please Thomson, the settler, who had chosen Rottnest to escape contact with Aborigines.[3] In August 1838 Constable Lawrence Welsh took ten prisoners to the Island. He received £75 per annum and a daily ration of one pound of flour and one pound of meat. He was instructed to erect suitable dwellings and to organise fishing and the collection of salt. No accommodation had been prepared. Initially the Aboriginal prisoners lived in a damp cave.

The penal settlement had an inauspicious start with seven of the ten prisoners escaping in Thomson's boat which had been left unsecured on the beach. One drowned before the escapees reached the mainland where the others were recaptured and returned to the Island.

When more prisoners were sent across, the Crown resumed all land on the Island with the exception of that in the name of a Major Bute, an absentee landlord. Thomson, Clarke and Lyon were rewarded with compensatory grants of land near the Swan River Settlement. Welsh (now a Corporal) left the Island in 1839 and was replaced by Henry Vincent, Gaoler, from Fremantle. He was a veteran of the Napoleonic Wars and had lost an eye at Waterloo. He is said to have been a man of limited intelligence, and harsh in the management of his charges. Thirty-six lashes were inflicted for attempting to escape. However, Vincent established crops of barley and vegetables (for his own household). Substantial buildings were constructed, roads and paths laid out, and work commenced on a lighthouse. Many of the buildings are now used for holiday accommodation.

The daily prison routine in the summer of 1842 was —

5.30 a.m. Cells unlocked and prisoners released to the open.

6.00 a.m. 6 men sent to cut grass, 2 to check fishing lines, 2 sharpened axes and one detailed to warm up breakfast (precooked the previous evening). Other chores included cutting wood, gathering stone for building, cow dung for the garden and thistles for the rabbits and pigs. If the tools were damaged, or the quality of the work poor, the order was 'No Breakfast", a sentence invariably received in sullen silence.

7.30 a.m.	After breakfast 12 men were employed grubbing land 6 digging the foundations of the lighthouse, 2 on home duties, and 2 more sent fishing.
3.00 p.m.	All prisoners returned to the depot.
4.30 p.m.	All were called to dinner which, like breakfast, was taken in absolute silence except for the scraping of bowls and sucking of fingers.[4]

After dinner the men were permitted to hold a short corroboree. Conversation must have been difficult as prisoners usually belonged to different tribal groups and had no common language.

The meals were monotonous in the extreme — 750 grams of oatmeal and 1 kilogram of cabbage per man, per day. There was a weekly issue of rice and an occasional ration of bread. The prisoners had Sunday free to hunt for meat, quokkas or snakes, or to catch fish.

The official Government penal concept originally was to teach the Aboriginal prisoners basic agricultural skills, in order, it was hoped, that they would have the option of using such skills after their ultimate release. In practice this was unsuccessful as they returned to an alien white society unwilling to offer and unable to give employment on any long term

Rottnest Island: An Island of Incarceration Leg irons, wrist shackles and chains used to fetter recalcitrant prisoners during their work outside the cells of the Quad. Photograph, courtesy of the Rottnest Island Museum, 1994, with acknowledgements.

Rottnest Island: An Island of Incarceration: During the period of the Aboriginal Prison on Rottnest Island (1838 – 1903), between five and ten prisoners slept in each cell with a floor area averaging 3 metres by 1.7 metres. This sculptured tableaux recreated by the Rottnest Island Museum, with acknowledgements

basis. After any brief seasonal work which was available, the Aborigines tended to return to their own people.

The crimes for which they were transported included tribal killings and sheep and cattle stealing; and occasionally simply the inability to conform to the white man's social regulations.

Colonial Engineer Trigg wrote, after a visit to Rottnest Island in 1842 —

> The prisoners will sit down and weep most bitterly, particularly the old men, or those who

> have left wives and children on the mainland; and when they see the smoke from the fires at the place where they have been accustomed to meet when unshackled and free, memory wanders over the scenes of bygone days. They seem sensitively alive to their lost freedom and lamentably bewail their captivity.[5]

Rottnest Island: An Island of Incarceration: The Quad, the central octagonal prison on Rottnest Island 18 km off the coast of Fremantle, in the Indian Ocean. The eight wings of this Prison for Aboriginal men contained cells designed for 106 prisoners, but held as many as 179. Photo, 1994.

Largely unable to communicate with one another, their plight was great. They were totally unable to adapt to their confinement.

Apart from the Sundays, the prisoners laboured for six days, often in chains, returning to their cells at night. The cells averaged 3 metres by 1.7 metres and held usually five, but sometimes up to ten prisoners.

Each prisoner was provided with one suit of clothes and one thin blanket in all weathers, sleeping on the floor of the cell. Rottnest winters are usually cold and very wet. Their diet was deficient in vegetables as attempts to grow them on the Island were only partially successful.

The octagonal prison, known as the Quad, was designed for 106 prisoners, but in one month of May it held 179. It is therefore not surprising that epidemics — influenza, measles, whooping cough, even the common cold — were lethal to this group of displaced and incarcerated men. In 1883 there were 70 deaths out of 100 prisoners, and of the total 3,400 who were transported to Rottnest Island between 1838 and 1902 at least 314 died. Aboriginal researchers claim that there were far more. The cause of death was predominantly pneumonia. A medical officer sailed from Fremantle on a regular basis; twenty-four visits were recorded in 1888. The doctor usually reported that sanitary conditions were good, food plentiful, and clothing warm and adequate. He concluded one official report by complaining bitterly of the six hour crossing, and of the lack of the long promised steamship for the passage! There were no nursing facilities whatsoever. Some of the larger rooms in the Quad were converted to hospital use but only the warders were available for nursing duties. There were usually a few white prisoners on the Island but never more than fifteen. They were skilled tradesmen, carpenters and masons. There was only one execution on Rottnest. Wanjebiddi was hanged in the presence of the other prisoners. His offence is not recorded.[6] A prisoner with a different story was John Lomas. He had a history of mental instability in England before his transportation in 1857 for setting fire to a barley stack. He was fifty-five when he arrived at the colony and for a year was confined to the Fremantle Lunatic Asylum. He received a conditional pardon in 1860 but was soon back behind bars for stealing a horse. He had a further break-down in prison and was described as "half-crazed and quite unfit to receive Ticket-of-Leave". Eventually he was removed to Rottnest Island as an Imperial Pauper, maintained by the Government. By 1870 he was allowed to visit the mainland for medical attention and

> ... to attend the solemnities of his Roman Catholic faith.

A cottage was built for John Lomas in the early 1870s and he received a daily ration of rum as a stimulant. The cottage was later occupied by Warden

Buckingham and is now known as Buckingham Palace. It is still standing. In 1888, aged eighty-six, Lomas was charged with vagrancy while visiting the mainland sent to Fremantle Gaol, and died soon after in the gaol hospital.[7]

Between 1849 and 1855 the prison was closed and the prisoners transferred to Fremantle. This was because acting Governor Hutt believed there was too much idleness on the Island. During this period it was leased by James Dempster for £80 per annum

Rottnest Island — An Island of Incarceration: An 1880 photograph of the prisoners and senior custodial staff (at right) at the Aboriginal Prison on Rottnest Island. Three years later, in 1883, seventy per one hundred prisoners died in a devastating epidemic. Photograph [No. 894, Rottnest File], courtesy of the Library Board of Western Australia, with grateful acknowledgements.

for farming until he left in 1853. With the advent of more convict transportation from England and the subsequent overcrowding at Fremantle Gaol, the Aboriginal prisoners were returned to Rottnest in 1855 under the old system. One unusual visitor to the Island in 1872 was the English novelist Anthony Trollope, but there seems no record of his observations.

A Boys' Reformatory was established in 1882 for no more than fourteen miscreants — at one time, only three. The youngest boy was eight, the oldest sixteen. Their offences were mainly thieving — cakes and pigeons are mentioned — and children who had been abandoned and were vagrants. The reformatory appears to have been a civilised establishment without draconian punishments. The boys were employed in the maintenance of buildings, painting and minor repairs, and received a good education with a qualified teacher. It was closed in 1901, the last fourteen boys being transferred to the Salvation Army Industrial School for Boys at Collie, a coal mining town 170 km south of Perth. The ultimate fate of any of the boys imprisoned at Rottnest Island has not been recorded.

During the First World War up to 1700 German, Austrian and Croatian internees or prisoners of war were held on Rottnest Island from August 1914 to November 1915 when they were transferred to internment camps in New South Wales. In the Second World War the Island was fortified with 9.2 inch guns, as part of the coastal defence, as there was real anxiety that Japanese troops would invade the southern coasts of Western Australia. Schoolchildren were evacuated from Perth, to supposedly safer country areas. However the expected Japanese invasion move south did not materialise, so there were no shots fired in anger. There were a small number of Italian prisoners of war on the Island performing menial tasks for the Army personnel.

A small number of prisoners served out their sentences until the 1920s, well after the closure of the prison, and the last prisoner was returned to the mainland in 1931. During its long existence the role of the establishment had changed from the vision of a training institution to a prison with a record of death, horror and despair unequalled by any other Aboriginal Prison in the Australian colonies.[8]

After the First World War the Island was developed as a holiday resort, and is now the most popular destination for Western Australian holiday-makers. Applications to stay far exceed the accommodation available. Rottnest provides all the recreations of summer; and accommodation ranges from tents in a camping area to flats, cottages, both the old buildings of Henry Vincent, and new ones designed to complement the past. There is also a Lodge, with an excellent restaurant, an hotel and fast food outlets. It is a popular venue for conferences, with all the audio–visual aids available.

As well as frequent ferry services, taking about forty minutes for the crossing, there is an hourly air service during daylight — the shortest commercial flight in the world — taking only ten to fifteen minutes.

Between 1948 and 1961 a pilot from the First World War, Captain Jimmy Woods, flew passengers in an Avro Anson. He was an indomitable character, with splendid disregard for weather conditions and for Department of Civil Aviation regulations. He was finally grounded by the D.C.A on the grounds of his age, sixty-eight, and his refusal to employ a co-pilot. He never lost a passenger.[9] Today the flight is faster and smoother, with some wonderful views. During the crossing one can see sharks, whales, dolphins and the reefs below.

In 1907, to prevent Rottnest Island being sold in 400 half acre subdivisions to the highest bidders, Governor Bedford declared the Island a public park and recreation forever, rather than the idea of —

> being exploited for the benefit of a few men who at this time could afford to buy or rent plots and build. The natural beauty of this island should not be disturbed more than is absolutely necessary.[10]

It was declared an A Class Reserve in 1917 and a Board of Control appointed, answerable now to the Minister of Tourism in Western Australia. On the Island itself the Rottnest Island Authority is responsible for the day to day management. A recent problem arose on Rottnest Island over the burial ground of the prisoners where it is certain that the 364 Aboriginal men must lie, although Aboriginal organisations believe there could be up to two thousand. As a result the authorities have relocated several small flats, and part of the camping area, known as Tentland to show respect to the former inmates incarcerated against their will.

Appropriate landscaping is proposed, and a suitable memorial with an Education Centre focussing on the plight of the Aboriginal People of Rottnest who died in shackles.

Rottnest Island — An Island of Incarceration: Cemeteries are one tangible record of the past. The Aboriginal Prisoners Cemetery on Rottnest Island rediscovered in 1984, has been duly re-signed as one page in the history of penology and its attempts, unsuccessful in the case of Rottnest Island to achieve concordance between two races in conflict. Photograph 1994.

Rottnest Island — An Island of Incarceration. The late twentieth century has brought an increasing awareness and acknowledgement of the history of the aboriginal peoples; and of European society's interaction with them. This photograph of 1994 records the existence of a nineteenth-century penal cemetery, hitherto forgotten and unacknowledged .

Peel Island

Quarantine as Incarceration

Peter Ludlow

efore the arrival of Europeans in Moreton. Bay, Peel Island was known to the Aborigines as Tukrooar or Chercuba. Its 400 hectares were insufficient to support a permanent tribe, but its abundance of marine life was a source of much feasting by visiting tribes from surrounding islands. Evidence of such occupation remains today in the form of extensive middens. The remnants of a bora ring indicates that the Island was also used for ceremonial purposes.

European migration in the mid-19th century brought contagious diseases such as cholera, typhoid, whooping cough, small-pox, measles, and consumption — outbreaks of which could decimate whole communities. Quarantine facilities were first established at Dunwich on Stradbroke Island in 1850, but the buildings were found to be more suitable as a Benevolent Asylum for aged and infirm members of the Moreton Bay Settlement. In 1865 an alternative Quarantine Station was built at St Helena Island using local prison labour, but after only a matter of months, the Queensland Government decided to convert the Island to a prison. This left the Quarantine Station to be returned to Dunwich to compete with the Benevolent Asylum for accommodation.

Finally the Government solved the problem by transferring the Quarantine Station to nearby Peel Island where in May 1874, the Island was proclaimed as such in lieu of Dunwich.

Peel's qualities were well suited to segregation: it had its own supply of fresh water; timber for fuel; and it was small enough to maintain control of its inmates and was surrounded by shark infested water to prevent escapes. It was close to Dunwich for supplies and for medical supervision from the Superintendent of the Benevolent Asylum; it was close to the main shipping channel into Brisbane; and it possessed a deep water anchorage for quarantined vessels.

The quarantine buildings stretched in a line along The Bluff on the Island's south-eastern corner, and commanded a magnificent view to the east across the short expanse of water towards Dunwich, across Moreton Bay. As on board ship, accommodation for passengers and crew was strictly segregated according to class. Saloon passengers occupied the largest building to the south. Next came the officers' quarters, doctor's quarters, and female steerage passengers. Crew and male steerage passengers slept in tents.

On Peel as on the voyage, the ship's Surgeon Superintendent was in charge of discipline as well as the health of the ship's passengers and crew. The following extract from a report made by Surgeon Superintendent J.L. Paddle of the barque *Southesk*, quarantined at Peel Island in 1882 indicates his considerable workload ... and his considerable powers:

> I beg further to report the following with reference to the general health and behaviour of the immigrants per ship '*Southesk*' while in Quarantine on Peel Island:
>
> They were landed on the island on May 13th [1882] and their chests on May 15th.
>
> I regret to report that 11 fresh cases of whooping cough occurred among the children since the ship anchored in Moreton Bay on May 10th including 3 cases since the passengers were landed ... The total number of cases of whooping cough on board and on the Island reached the number of 20.
>
> There were no fresh cases of measles or typhoid fever among the passengers while on the Island ...
>
> 4 deaths occurred on the Island among the patients suffering from whooping cough ...
>
> All the cases of whooping cough, when located, were placed in the special hospital for females, but as there was no room for all the cases in that

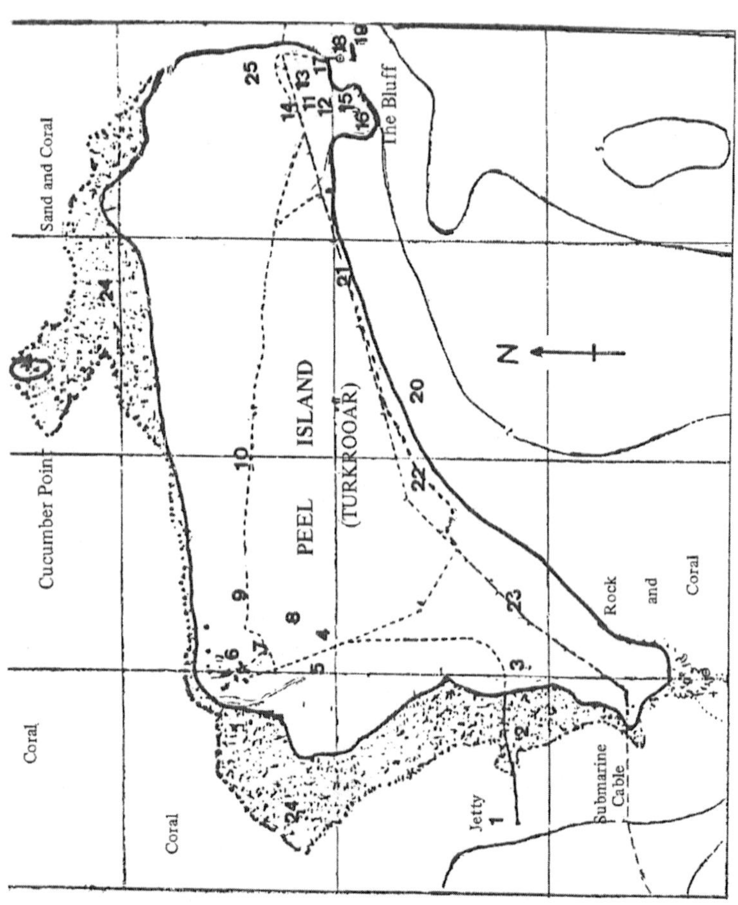
Sand and Coral
Cucumber Poin
Coral
Coral
PEEL ISLAND
(TURKROOAR)
The Bluff
Jetty
Submarine Cable
Rock and Coral
N

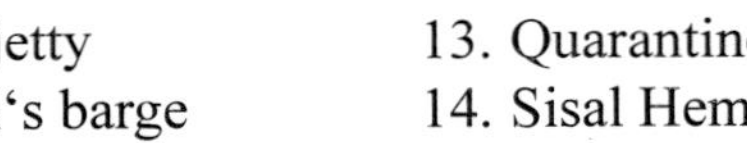

KEY TO PEEL ISLAND MAP

1. Western jetty
2. Surawski's barge
3. Pine grove
4. Freshwater swamp
5. Western jetty track
6. Lazaret buildings
7. Store and stables
8. Wells
9. Lazaret cemetery
10. Central track
11. Cell block
12. Site of quarantine station and Inebriate Home
13. Quarantine well
14. Sisal Hemp grove
15. Ranger's hut
16. The Bluff
17. Site of storage shed
18. Stone jetty
19. "Platypus"
20. Horseshoe Bay
21. Kiosk
22. Beach track
23. Former PMG line
24. Mangroves
25. Original quarantine cemetery

Peel Island- An Island of Quarantine Incarceration: A plan of Peel Island in Moreton Bay in south-east Queensland. A settlement established on the south-east corner of the Island (Features 11 to 19) housed a Quarantine Station (from 1874 until 1910); and a court-imposed Inebriate Asylum (from 1910 until 1916). A Government Lazaret (Features 5 to 9) was the enforced home of diagnosed sufferers of Hansen s Disease in the period from 1907 until 1959.

house, the 3 or 4 remaining cases were placed with their parents in small tents.

Peel Island: An Island of Quarantine Incarceration: An aerial photograph of Peel Island in Moreton Bay in south-east Queensland taken from the west looking eastward. Stradbroke Island is on the horizon. Horseshoe Bay is on the right. Photograph courtesy of the late Mr Marian Opala and Mrs Rosemary Opala, with acknowledgements.

Besides the cases of whooping cough, several cases of bronchitis occurred while on the Island. These I attributed to the very draughty state of the houses in which the immigrants were lodged ... I am of the opinion that the last 3 deaths were hastened, if not caused, by the very draughty and leaky state of the hospital. In wet and windy weather, the rain would enter through every chink, and it was really difficult to keep the houses dry ...

There were also a few slight cases of diarrhoea which I could refer to the same cause as those of bronchitis.

Several other cases were produced by change of diet from salt to fresh provisions. I received many complaints from the immigrants with reference to the quarantine rations, which consist of 1 lb of fresh meat, 1 lb of bread, and a few small extras. The majority informed me that they had never been accustomed to fresh meat (living mainly on porridge and farinaceous food) and that it disagreed with them. The 1 lb of meat they thought was more than they could manage, while they had not enough bread. I would accordingly beg to suggest that 1 ½ lb of bread and 3/4 lb of fresh meat would be considered, at any rate by Scotch Immigrants, as a more suitable allowance while in quarantine.

The provisions were supplied from Dunage [Dunwich] by the Superintendent of Quarantine and on one or two occasions they were forwarded from Town.

Some stores and medical comforts as well as medicines were landed from the '*Southesk*'; while a few additional drugs required were supplied by the Superintendent of Quarantine.

The Immigrants, on the whole, behaved very well on the Island and gave little trouble. The single women had to be closely watched all the time, as they had a great tendency to wander beyond their limits. At dusk they were ordered in and mustered to make sure that none were absent. I would further beg to suggest that it would greatly lighten the work of the Matron and the Constables in watching the single women, if a fence could be erected around their precincts.

One of the single women, Elizabeth Morris, gave much trouble one night, and I reported her to the Immigration Officer. On Monday evening May 22nd she gave a good deal of abuse to the Matron and kept swearing and cursing among the single women and inciting them to riot. She has been all along a very coarse and vulgar woman and very little amenable to authority throughout the voyage.

The Constables I appointed on the island were the same as those who had held these posts on board ship. I found it necessary to appoint 3 cooks on shore, for the single women, married men, and single men respectively. As the duties of the water closet constable were very heavy with the dry earth system used on the Island I appointed a second man to help him, Most of the Immigrants did not understand the workings of the earth closets, in spite of notices posted up in

each, and in consequence they were not kept as clean as they might have been. Daily inspections were, however, made and the boxes removed as frequently as possible.

As soon as the chests were landed they were all opened on the beach and their contents well exposed to the air. The single women's boxes were taken to their quarters to prevent any communication with the others and they aired their clothes on the grass in front of their houses.

The clothes and blankets of the Immigrants were also thoroughly washed with marine and carbolic soap.

On board the '*Southesk*', all the fittings were taken down and burnt and the ship thoroughly cleaned, lime-washed, and fumigated. I inspected her with the Superintendent of Quarantine on May 18th and gave a certificate to that effect. She was released from quarantine on May 22nd and towed up to the bar. The Immigrants were released from Quarantine on May 27th and taken to Brisbane in the 'Kate' on the same day.

In all, 78 ships were quarantined in Queensland last century. During the 1860s there were 20; in the seventies 24; in the eighties 31; but in the 1890s there were only 3. Thus by the turn of the century, Peel's quarantine buildings were largely disused.

Peel Island — An Island of Quarantine Incarceration: Quarantined passengers bathing at Peel Island in Moreton Bay, Queensland. Their ship, the '*Dorunda*' is offshore anchored near Bird Island. Photograph, 1885, courtesy of the Royal Historical Society of Queensland with acknowledgements.

Across the water at Dunwich, however, the Benevolent Asylum was very much overcrowded. A certain amount of relief was obtained in 1904 by transferring 40 of the strongest male patients across to the quarantine buildings at Peel Island. In addition about 80 acres of timber in the vicinity of the Station were cleared for grazing purposes, and a further 24 acres for the cultivation of crops for the use of the Benevolent Asylum inmates. However, after several years of essaying such crops as sweet potatoes, pumpkins, oats, barley, lucerne, Kaffir corn, and cow peas, the results proved most discouraging, owing to the extremely poor quality of the soil on that part of the Island. Even the Sisal Hemp, previously imported from the Bahamas and propagated by the prisoners at St Helena, proved to be very slow growing, although Dr Row did concede that there probably would ultimately be some slight return from it.

By 1910, the number of ships requiring isolation at Peel Island had diminished, and the wooden buildings were left unoccupied. It was then, following trouble with the inebriate inmates at the Benevolent Asylum in Dunwich, that the Government approved their use as an Inebriate Asylum. George Jackson was appointed as Chief Attendant and looked after the male inebriates. His wife, Agnes, as Matron, attended to the females. All the patients were white.

Dr Linford Row, Medical Superintendent of the Dunwich Benevolent Asylum, was also responsible for the well-being of the Inebriates on Peel. When the Inebriate Asylum took over in 1910, the male inebriates occupied the former female steerage passengers' quarters to the north, and the female inebriates the officers' quarters to the south. A high corrugated iron fence around the men's quarters was a remnant from the quarantine days, built to prevent contact between the single girls and the more eligible male passengers.

People were sent to the Inebriate Asylum to dry out. There were two types of patients: public and private. Private patients, or their relatives, had to pay

One Guinea ($ 2.10) a week for board and lodgings. Public patients had to earn their keep by working.

Peel Island — A Quarantine Island of Incarceration: An 1885 scene on Peel Island in Moreton Bay off the coast of south-east Queensland. This photograph shows some of the crew and passengers of the '*Dorunda*' incarcerated on the Island whilst the ship was quarantined offshore. The scene shows the saloon dining room with its wide verandahs, with the brick kitchen at the rear, left. Single men lived in tents, foreground right. Photograph, December 1885, courtesy of the Royal Historical Society of Queensland with acknowledgements.

As well as performing basic chores, patients were encouraged to make furniture or work in the mattress factory. This latter was situated at the back of the stone jetty below the Asylum. It consisted of a large wooden shed through which could be driven a horse and cart.

Grass collected from the Island was unloaded on to a platform on one side of the shed ready to be stuffed into mattresses. When completed, these were stored on a platform on the other side. Later they would be sent to Dunwich for the use of the aged men and women at the Benevolent Asylum.

Once a stray spark ignited the grass in the shed and the whole building was consumed. The building was totally destroyed, leaving only a few charred stumps for posterity, some of which still remain to this day.

George Jackson was of the belief that work kept people out of trouble. A master with a scythe, he trained many patients in the use of this cumbersome instrument. By their labours, the many hectares of grass surrounding the Asylum were always kept well cut.

There were 16 toilets at the Asylum, each with its own W.C. pan. The regular emptying and burying of their contents was not the most favoured job. Indeed, for the unsteady patient, it could be decidedly risky! Eventually, in 1912, the inmates revolted and refused to perform this most necessary chore. They demanded that outside labour be brought in to perform this unpleasant task. The Chief Attendant responded by withdrawing the patients' rations of tobacco, butter, and breakfast meat, and by locking the offending inmates in the corrugated iron enclosure of the men's compound. One private patient who at the time was having trouble meeting his weekly payments was also locked in with the 20 offending inmates. Their foul language caused him to write to his relatives for the necessary money to release him from "this most awful degraded Hell I can imagine darkening God's earth". Fortunately his relatives supplied the necessary cash.

The Quarantine Station had its own telegraph office from which daily medical reports could be sent to Dunwich. Later,

when the Inebriate Asylum took over the buildings, the telegraph was dismantled. This left the Asylum out of contact with Dunwich, on Stradbroke Island. For possible emergencies, a rifle was always left loaded and ready for use just outside the door of the Jacksons' house.

A couple of quick shots would attract the attention of the authorities at Dunwich just across the water, and help would be sent by boat. Fortunately, the rifle was never fired. The Inebriate Asylum operated for seven years from 1910 until 1916. At that point, the inmates were returned to the Benevolent Asylum at Dunwich, and the wooden buildings demolished.

Of all its exiles, Peel Island will be associated mostly with its leprosy patients. For them, their internment was not just for weeks or for months, but was for years and often for a lifetime. A visit to Peel was a journey into oblivion and forgottenness. A place of the leper where identity changed to protect the family name; a place of stigma and of dread. Leprosy, or Hansen's Disease as it is more kindly known today, came into Queensland with the immigrant influx to the gold fields in the mid-nineteenth century. Spreading quickly through the native Aboriginal Peoples and the South Sea Islanders ('kanakas') imported to work the sugar cane fields, the disease had become a sufficient threat to the white population by 1893 for the Government to introduce the Leprosy Act of that year. This made Leprosy a notifiable disease where the unfortunate patient was obliged by law to be segregated for treatment in designated lazarets. Aboriginal and Chinese victims were incarcerated on Friday Island off the coast of Cape York, and at Dunwich for the whites.

The Dunwich lazaret was attached to the Benevolent Asylum and the patients shared the same facilities. However, when it was discovered that the postmaster's son had contracted Leprosy after participating in concerts to entertain the combined inmates, it was quickly decided to move the Lazaret over to Peel Island where it opened in 1907 on the north-western corner of the island.

The Peel Lazaret was perhaps Queensland's first truly multicultural community, for within its small confines were Chinese, Aborigines, South Sea Islanders, and whites of both European and Australian origin. They were housed in four compounds: white males, white females, "coloured males", and "coloured females". The whites had individual wooden huts, as did the coloured women, but the coloured men were housed, four to a hut, in constructions of corrugated iron on a cement slab.

Patient numbers were to peak at 86. The majority were Aboriginal or Chinese men and women. Peel Island lazaret was unique in Australia in that so many whites were infected as well. To care for the patients, about thirty staff were employed. These included attendants, cooks, housekeepers and a superintendent. Medical visits were on a weekly basis from the Superintendent of the Benevolent Asylum at Dunwich, and later by visiting Government Medical Officers on a monthly basis, weather permitting.

Although not prisoners in the accepted sense, nevertheless, Peel's leprosy patients were not permitted to return to the mainland or their homes. Two visitors' passes per month were issued to family members. This permitted an hour's exchange between the patient and his family on Peel's stone jetty while the supply boat swapped cargo at Dunwich. No contact was allowed and children under the age of 14 were not permitted ashore.

Because they could not be dealt with as prisoners and confined or flogged for their misdemeanour's, unruly patient behaviour was controlled by either refusing to issue visitor passes, or by threatening to send the police around to the offender's relatives and thus "get the neighbours' tongues wagging".

Once segregated on Peel Island the patients were confronted with the problem of how to amuse themselves. In 1911, the Government had provided a boat for the patients to fish the surrounding reefs. This also provided the more restless patients with a means of escape. After several such attempts, an officer from the Health Department visited the settlement one night in September 1913 and burnt all the boats. Two police officers accompanied him just in case there were reprisals from the patients. This incident would never be forgotten and memory of it was passed down over the decades. Although the rules were gradually relaxed in time and patients were again allowed to have their own boats, the threatened repetition of the burning would be used against prospective escapees even into the 1940s.

New treatments were always being developed in various parts of the world in the hope of curing Leprosy. Many were of little benefit and some smacked of out-and-out quackery. However all were taken seriously by the patients who were desperate to find a cure for the debilitating and disfiguring ailment which was the cause of their incarceration. When news arrived at Peel Island that a new form of treatment had been developed by a certain Deycha Pacha called the Nastin Treatment, they were keen to act as guinea pigs. The Government concurred and ordered all the required medical supplies. In due course these arrived and the Nastin Treatment was commenced on Peel Island on May 18th, 1909.

One of the requirements for patients undertaking the Nastin Treatment was that they take no alcohol, so their daily ration of half a bottle of beer or 2 oz of spirits was withheld. To the average drinker such abstention presented no problem, but one of the patients, Rose Harris (her pseudonym) was an agitator determined to make the Government regret ever placing her in detention on Peel. In addition, she had been an alcoholic for a long time prior to her admission to the lazaret. Until the commencement of the Nastin Treatment, she had managed to maintain her supplies of alcohol by trading her favours for a man's daily beer ration.

Although the women patients were padlocked in their compound each night behind a four metre high wire fence, religious services for the mixed sexes were held nightly between 7.30 and 8.30 p.m. It was here that Rose had been able to solicit her menfolk. Trouble began when the men on the Nastin Treatment were no longer given their beer ration and therefore could not supply Rose with her alcoholic requirements. Being a scheming and manipulative person, she realised that the only way to regain her liquid requirements was to have the Nastin Treatment stopped. This she did by convincing some of the men patients that Dr Row was not handling the treatment properly. Consequently, when faced with a deputation that he supply the patients with written instructions on the Nastin Treatment, the doctor refused. This resulted in the deputation of patients refusing any further such treatment from Dr Row and demanding that he allow

another doctor to give it instead. This request he also refused. Three of the patients, however, still wished to receive the treatment — until they were threatened with bodily harm if they didn't join Rose Harris and her followers. They had little choice.

Faced with open rebellion by his patients, prostitution, alcoholism, and threats of bodily harm, Dr Row sought help from the Government. The official inquiry called for the patients to come forward and give evidence. Once again the patients were divided — some made an official statement and some did not. From those who did, however, the whole story emerged and pointed to Rose Harris as the troublemaker. To avoid any further problems, it was recommended that all women patients be transferred to a separate lazaret to be built at Dunwich. This recommendation was condemned by the Government and the women remained at the lazaret on Peel, but under much closer supervision. The central personality, Rose Harris, was to die in 1912, and her grave is still to be seen in the lazaret's little cemetery amongst the gum trees.

And the Nastin Treatment? Suffice it to relate that the Queensland Health Department's Annual Report of 1910 simply states that it was a failure at Peel Island.

More trouble was to emerge in 1921 when the Health Officer was called to investigate reports of unrest in the "coloured compound". He concluded that it had all been due to three ring-leaders, part Aboriginal men who, in his opinion, thought that being Leprosy patients put them outside the law. Alcohol was the main problem, which although officially denied to the coloureds, was being brought in and buried either by staff members returning from leave, or by friends. White patients wrote to the Government expressing fears of murder, especially for the white women, and demanded police protection. A magistrate and two police officers visited the island and two revolvers were confiscated.

It was no easy task to overcome the inherent monotony of daily life on Peel Island. For this reason, the Government encouraged all able bodied patients to engage in manual labour, for which they were paid a reasonable wage. Such duties involved the maintenance of the 5 km of roadway on the Island as well as cementing, carpentry repairs, and erection of new cottages. The spread of prickly pear had also been a problem at Peel as it had been in the rest of Queensland. After being cleared by outside labour in 1923, regrowth was kept under control by the patients themselves. Those not willing or able to work indulged in gardening, fishing, bathing, and playing sports, or if these amusements were

too “physical” listening to gramophone records or in reading the books and magazines donated by the members of the public.

From the 1920s, visits from patients’ relatives were encouraged by the issue of free rail passes to those living in remote areas, while for those relatives left in poor circumstances by the segregation of their breadwinner, suitable employment was found. The spiritual needs of the patients were catered for by frequent visits from Ministers of Religion of all denominations, while their stomachs received a morale boost with the construction of a new and better appointed kitchen in 1927. In addition, a resident nurse was appointed in 1925 to handle day to day emergencies. The greatest innovation was the installation of a loudspeaker wireless in 1925. Then, for the first time, patients had direct contact with the outside world, if only from the receiving end.

Its popularity with the patients can be gauged by the many thousands of carbon cell batteries which powered their radios over the years, and which now litter the embankment to the north of the men’s compound. So, by the time the Lazaret entered Its third decade, life there had progressed a long way from the lawlessness of its first years. Although still primitive by modern standards, life there did have its compensations. Indeed, all concerned with the Island began to feel some consolation in knowing that the “bad old days” of the Lazaret were finally over. With the steady increase in patient numbers during the 1930s, it was finally decided to shift the non white patients, who were all Aborigines by this time, to Fantome Island off Townsville. This occurred in 1940 and left only white patients at Peel Island.

With the advent of World War II, Government material and staff resources were stretched to the limit. Perhaps rightly, the patients felt that their needs had been forgotten. In the early 1940s a “new breed” of patients began to be admitted to Peel. These were young active men without family ties who were not prepared to accept the conditions they found there. Bolstered by a donation of £200 from an Anglican newspaper, a Patients’ Committee “fighting fund” was set up.

With the Lazaret’s only telephone restricted to staff use, the Committee was restricted to letter writing which it did with a vengeance to the newspapers, to the Queensland State Health Department and Minister for Health. A delegation of eight patients tried to sail to the mainland to present their grievances to the newspapers and the Health Department in person but bad weather forced them back. However they were more successful in sending a patient to Canberra to see the Commonwealth Health Minister. Although they did not receive the Royal Commission they sought, they received much valuable publicity.

The patients’ resentment to the staff’s freedoms was further fuelled by the purchase of a truck for transport to the jetty at the other end of the Island. Staff could use the truck while patients still had to use the horse and dray. One day, the dray broke down *en route* and mysteriously caught fire. The Patients' Committee had struck again!

In 1947 conditions were greatly improved by the introduction of two diesel powered electricity generators. Each cabin was lit at the flick of a switch. There were street lights and even movies twice a week in the recreation hall. But 1947 was more memorable for the introduction of Promin, the first of the sulphone drugs which were to provide a cure for Leprosy. During the 1950s the patient numbers gradually fell. In 1959 Peel Island as an island of incarceration, was closed down and the remaining nine patients transferred to the South Brisbane Hospital.

Although leprosy had been cured on Peel, its stigma still remained and the Government's efforts to sell off the empty buildings as a fitness camp or resort were unsuccessful. Thirty years were to pass before the public's curiosity overcame its fear. Tours visited the island in increasing numbers over the next few years, until in 1993 the Queensland Government decided to gazette the Lazaret a Heritage area and the rest of the Island a future National Park.

NOTES AND REFERENCES

Chapter 1

1. **Forsyth WG**. *Govenor Arthur's Convict System. Van Diemen's Land 182 1 1824-36. A Study in Colonization.* London, Longmans, Green and Co., 1935:85

2. **Pink, Kerry.** Through Hell's Gates — A History of Strahan and Macquarie Harbour, Burnie (Tasmania), *The Advocate* Newspaper, 1984:31

3. **3 Historical Records of Australia**. HRA 3; iii: 19. Letter from Governor Sorell, at Hobart, to Goulburn, dated 12 May 1820

4. **Historical Records of Australia**. HRA 3; *v*: 346. Letter from Governor Arthur, at Hobart, to Hay, 4 September 1826

5. **Julen, Hans**. *The Penal settlement of Macquarie Harbour*. Launceston (Tasmania), Regal Publications, 1988: 5,12.

6. **Ibid**: 7,10.

7. **Lempriere, Thomas James**. The Penal Settlements of Early Van Diemen's Land [1839]. Facsimile Ed. [1954]. Hobart, *Roy Soc Tas,* 1954:47.

Chapter 1 (contd)

8. **Brand Ian**. *Sarah Island Penal Settlements 1822-1833 and 1846-1847.* Launceston (Tasmania), Regal Publications, 1990:

9. **Pearn J**. *In the Capacity of a Surgeon.* Brisbane, Amphion Press, 1988. Ch.5-7: 57-116.

10. **Pearn J**. Surgeon Emile Deplanche. Scientist and doctor of the South Pacific. *Med J. Aust* 1994; 160: 568-571.

11. **Macfie, Peter**. Medicine and Health at the Port Arthur Penal Colony. Invited Address, The Australian Society of the History of Medicine. Biennial Conference, Hobart, 1993.

12. **Historical Records of Australia**. HRA III: vi: 102, Letter, dated 12th April 1827 from Surgeon John Barnes to Governor Arthur.

13. **Archives HM Public Records Office [London]** CO280/28 pp.296-299.

14. **Evans GW**. Report of Deputy Surveyor-General GW Evans to Lieutenant Governor Colonel William Sorell, of Hobart Town, 1822. Tasmanian State Archives.

15. **Munro D**. From Port Macquarie Harbour to Port Arthur: the founding of a penal settlement. Tas His RES Assoc. Papers and Proceedings 1989; 36(3): 113-124.

Chapter 2.

1. **Fidion PG, Ryan RJ**. Eds. *The Journal of Phillip Gidley King; Lieutenant, RN. 1787-1790*. Sydney: Australian Documents Library, 45.

2. **Hazzard M.** *Punishment Short of Death: A History of the Penal Settlement at Norfolk Island.* Melburne: Hyland House, 1984: 12.

3. **Rigg V**. Convict Life: A 'tolerable degree of comfort.? **In**: R, ed. *Norfolk Island and its first Settlement, 1788-1814*. North Sydney: Library of Australian History, 1988: 97.

4. **Ibid**, 99.

5. **Historical Records of New South Wales** (hereafter **H.R.N.S.W.**) Vol 1, Part 2, 441.

6. **H.R.N.S.W.**, Vol 3, 159.

7. **H.R.N.S.W.**, Vol 2, 18.

8. **H.R.N.S.W.**, Vol 6, 138.

9. **Pearn JH**. Courage and Curiosity: Surgeon-Explorers in Australia and New Zealnd, Part 1. Discovery and Bridgehead. *Australian and New Zealand Journal of Surgery,* 1992; 32:227.

Chapter 2 (contd)

10. **H.R.N.S.W.**, Vol 3, 44.

11. **H.R.N.S.W.**, Vol 2, 250.

12. **Fidion PG & RYAN RJ**, *op.cit.*, 326.

13. **H.R.N.S.W.**, Vol 3, 161.

14. **King PG**. *Journal of Transactions on Norfolk Island* Nov.4, 1791-Nov.6, 1794, 40.

15. **Ibid**. 66-67.

16. **Ibid**. 66-67.

17. **H.R.N.S.W.**, Vol 3, 24.

18. **Historical Records of Australia**, Series 1, (hereafter H.R.A.), Vol 2, 569.

19. **King PG**, *op.cit.*, 329.

20. **King PG**, *op.cit.*, 590-91.

21. **H.R.A.** Vol 1, 539.

22. **H.R.N.S.W.**, Vol 3, 451.

23. **H.R.A.**, Vol 5, 480-81.

24. **Ibid**, 481.

25. **Ibid**, 482.

Chapter 2 (contd)

26. **Foveaux, Joseph**. Letter Book 16 November 1800 — 7 September 1804,43.

27. **H.R.N.S.W.**, Vol6, 741,757.

28. **H.R.N.S.W.**, Vol5, 552.

29. **H.R.A.**, Vol6, 647.

30. **H.R.N.S.W.**, Vol7, 366.

31. **Ibid.**

32. **H.R.N.S.W.**, Vol6, 138.

33. **Hoare, Merval**. *Norfolk Island An Outline of its History, 1774-1977*.University of Queensland Press, 1978: 31-34.

34. **H.R.A.**, Vol13, 36.

35. **Quoted from A.G.L. Shaw**, Convicts and the Colonies, (Faber and Faber London, 1966), in Rigg V, Convict Life : 'a planned and unrelenting exclusion of happiness and comforts'. **In**: Nobbs R, ed. *Norfolk Island and its Second Settlement 1825-1855*. North Sydney: Library of Australian History, 1988: 17.

Chapter 2 (contd)

36. **Quoted from A. Price**, History of Norfolk Island from Discovery in 1774 to Present Day, MS, Dixon Library, 2. in Rigg, Convict Life: 'a planned and unrelenting exclusion of happiness and comforts'. **In**: Nobbs R, ed. *Norfolk Island and its Second Settlement 1825-1855*. North Sydney Library of Australian History, 1988: 18.

37. **Quoted from Charles White**, Early Australian History: Convict Life in New South Wales and Van Diemen's Land Parts I and 11, (Bathurst: C & GS White, 'Free Press' Office, 1889), 282, in Treadgold, M. Economic Development. *In*: Nobbs R, ed. *Norfolk Island and its Second Settlement* 1825-1855. North Sydney: Library of Australian History, 1988: 77.

38. **Mortlock JF**, *Experiences of a Convict*, Sydney University Press, 1965, 65.

39. **Cook T**, *The Exile's Lamentations*. North Sydney: Library of Australian History, 1978: 61.

40. **Stuart RP, Naylor TB**. Norfolk Island 1846: *The Botany Bay of Botany Bay*. Sullivan's Cove, 1979: 38-39.

41. **Martin E, Cox P**. Rebuilding the Settlement. In: Nobbs R, ed. *Norfolk Island and its Second Settlement, 1825-1855*. North Sydney: Library of Australian History, 1988: *op.cit*., 107-8.

Chapter 2 (contd)

42. Martin E, Cox P. Rebuilding the Settlement. In: Nobbs R, ed. *Norfolk Island and its Second Settlement, 1825-1855*. North Sydney: Library of Australian History, 1988: 115-116.

43. Hazzard,*op.cit.*, 124.

44. Mortlock, *op.cit.*, 66.

45. Quoted from A.G.L. Shaw, Convicts and the Colonies, (Faber and Faber London, 1966) 249, in Rigg V, Convict Life: 'a planned and unrelenting exclusion of happiness and comforts'. **In**: Nobbs R, ed. *Norfolk Island and its Second Settlement 1825-1855*. Nrth Sydney: Library of Australian History, 1988: 17.

46. Cook, *op.cit.*, 62.

47. Ibid.

48. Rev. Thomas Atkins, *Reminiscences of 12 Years Residence in Tasmania and NewSouth Wales*. Malvern: 1869:27,28.

49. Bunbury, *Reminiscences of a Veteran*. London: Skeet, 1861: 2, 301-2 .

50. H.R.A., Vol17, 638.

Chapter 2 (contd)

51. **Ullathorn WB**. *Autobiography of Archbishop Ullathom, with Extracts from His Letters*. London : Burns and Oats, 100.

52. **Quoted from Waiter Clay**, The Prison Chaplain. A Memoir of the Rev.John Clay, London 1861: 44, in Myers A. Alexander Maconochie. In: Nobbs R, ed. *Norfolk Island and its Second Settlement, 1825-1855*. North Sydney: Library of Australian History, 1988: 65.

53. **Annual Return of Diseases treated civil hospitals in Norfolk Island** (JV Thompson, MS REP. April 1841).

54. **Rogers T**. Correspondence Relating to the Dismissal ofThe Rev. TRogers from His Chaplaincy at Norfolk Island. Launceston: 1848: 97-8.

55. **Ibid**, 101.

Chapter 3.

1. **'The Plan of Port Cockbum'**, insert to JW Norie, North Pacific Ocean — New Guinea, ML Ref ZM3 921/1821/10.

2. **Colonial Secretary Macleay to Major Lockyer**, 1826, HRA, Series I, V *xii,* p453.

Chapter 3 (contd)

3. **Earl Bathurst to Sir Thomas Brisbane** 17 02 .1824, HRA, Series III, V *v*, p758.

4. **Government Public Notice** 1102.1824, HRA, Series Ill, V *vi*, p643 0

5. **Captain Bremer to Secretary Croker**, August 1824, HRA, Series III, V *xi*, p765.

6. **Captain Bremer to Secretary Croker** 11.11.1824, HRA, Series I, V *xi*, p769.

7. **'View of Fort Dundas'**, from PP King, *Survey of the Intertropical Coasts of Australia*, Vol11, ML Ref C 966 opp.p237.

8. **Earl Bathurst to Sir Thomas Brisbane** 702.1824, HRA, Series III, V *v*, p758.

9. **Mr G Miller to Secretary Harrison** 9.11.1824, HRA, Series III, V v, p768.

10. **Captain Bremer to Secretary Croker** 11.11.1824, HRA, Series III, V *v*, p769.

11. **Colonial Secretary Macleay to Major Lockyer** 1826, HRA, Series I, V *xii*, p453.

12. **New South Wales Government Archives**, Return of Sick at Melville Island 1.11.1824-30.4.1825, Series 4/1802, Reel 6066, p 57-62.

13. **Captain Barlow to Major Owens** 19.05.1825, HRA, Series III, V *vi,* p645.

Chapter 3 (contd)

14. J Campbell, Geographical Memoir of Melville Island and Port Essington, P*roceedings of the Royal Geographical Society of London*, 1834, p150.

15. Dr Turner to Major Ovens 25.5.1825, HRA, Series III, V *vi*, p650.

16. Captain Barlow to Major Ovens 27.8.1825, HRA, Series III, V *vi*,p651.

17. Colonel Dumaresq to Captain Barlow 28.11.1825, HRA, Series Ill, V *vi*, p653.

18. J Campbell, The British Settlement of Fort Dundas on Melville Island 24.4.1827, NSW Archives Authority Ref map 2 no. 8054.

19. BD Reid, Malaria in the Nineteenth Century British Military Settlements, *Journal of Northern Territory History*, 1992, p 41·54.

20. Major Campbell to Colonial Secretary Macleay 7.6.1827, HRA, Series III, V *vi*. p696.

Chapter 3 (contd)

21. **Major Campbell to Colonial Secretary Macleay** 20.6.1828, HRA, Series III, V *vi,* p721.

22. **Captain Hartley to Colonial Secretary Macleay** 20.6.1828, HRA, Series III, V *vi*, p729.

23. **Captain Hartley to Colonial Secretary Macleay** 8.9.1828, HRA, Series III, V vi, p757.

24. **J Campbell**, Geographical Memoir of Melville Island and Port Essington, *Proceedings of the Royal Geographical Society of London*, 1834, p151.

25. **J Mulvaney and N Green** (Eds), *The Journals of Captain Collet Barker 1828-1831*, Melbourne University Press, 1992, p157.

26. **JT Bigge**, State of NSW, p 125, in CMH Clark, *Select Documents in Australian History* 1788-1850, Angus and Robertson, Sydney, 1950, p136.

Chapter 4.

1. **Steel JG**. 1975. B*risbane Town in convict days, 1824-1842*. (University of Queensland Press: Brisbane) 403 pp.

2. **Bateson C**. 1966. Patrick Logan, tyrant of Brisbane Town. (Ure Smith: Sydney) 190 pp.

3. **Pearn JH**. 1988. *In the Capacity of a Surgeon.* A biography of Walter Scott, surgeon and Australian colonist, and first civilian of Queensland. (The University of Queensland: Brisbane) 226 pp.

Chapter 4 (contd)

4. **St Pierre J**. 1994. *Moreton Bay detachment 1824-25*. The soldiers who served at the Redcliffe convict settlement. (The Redcliffe Historical Society Inc: Redcliffe) 70 pp.

5. **Durbridge E & Covacevich J**. 1981. *North Stradbroke Island.* (Stradbroke Management Organization, Point Lookout, North Stradbroke Island) 168 pp.

6. **O'Keefe M**. 1975. Some aspects of the history of Stradbroke Island.*Proceedings of the Royal Society of Queensland* 86(15): 85-89.

7. **Cranfield L**. 1964. Early commandants of Moreton Bay. *Journal of the Royal Historical Society of Queensland* 7(2): 385 -398.

8. **Craig WW**. 1925. Moreton Bay Settlement or Queensland before Separation 1770-1859 together with a brief account of the rise of the colonies of Australasia. (Watson, Ferguson & Co. Ltd: Brisbane) 125 pp.

9. **Brazier RF**. 1920. Nfolk Island. *Journal of the Historical Society of Queensland* 2(1): 27A5.

10. **Hoare M**. 1972. Norfolk Island. An outline of its history 1774-1968. (University of Queensland Press: Brisbane).

Chapter 4 (contd)

11. **Hazzard M**. 1978. 'Convicts and commandants of Norfolk Island 1788-1855'. (Photocopies International: Norfolk Island) 57 pp.

12. **Covacevich JA, Ogilvie A, & Walker F**. (in press). 'Stone walls do not a prison make ... ' Profiles of prisoners of North Stradbroke Island Queens- land Australia. *Proceedings of the Australian Society of the History of Medicine Conference*, Mutiny and Medicine, Norfolk Island 2-9 July,1995.

13. **Pearce C**. 1994. *Through the eyes of Thomas Pamphlett, convict and castaway*. (Boolarong Publications: 12 Brookes St., Bowen Hills, Brisbane.

14. **Carter P, Durbridge E. & Cooke-Bramley J**. (eds) 1994. *North Stradbroke Island*. (North Stradbroke Island Historical Museum Association Inc: Dunwich) 168 pp.

Chapter 5.

1. **Campbell FJ**. Cockatoo (Biloela) Island. *Journal of Royal Australian Historical Society*, Vol 18, 1932, op 338-9.

2. **Stephensen PR**. *The History and Description of Sydney Harbour*, p 240.

3. **Despatch 102 from Gipps**, *Historical Records of Australia* Series I, Vol 24, p 86.

Chapter 5 (contd)

4. **Campbell FJ**, *op.cit.*, pp 339-340.

5. **Gipps' Despatch**, HRA Series I, Vol 24, pp 85-86.

6. **Gipps to Stanley**, HRA Series I, Vol 24, p 611.

7. **FitzRoy to Earl Grey**, HRA Series I, Vol 25.

8. **FitzRoy to Earl Grey**, HRA Series I, Vol 26 p 328.

9. **Bishop Davis**, Colonial Secretary Correspondence, Archives Office New South Wales 4/2431 50.6334.

10. Medical Adviser, Colonial Secretary Correspondence, Archives Office New South Wales 4/245 3 52.9274.

11. Medical Adviser, Colonial Secretary Correspondence, Archives Office New South Wales 4/2460 53.8622.

12. Visiting Magistrate, Colonial Secretary Correspondence, Archives Office New South Wales 4/2476 55.7642.

13. **Pendrill**, Report from the Inquiry into the Management of Cockatoo Island Appendices A toE, 1858 p 64.

14. **Peers**, Report ... Management Cockatoo Island pp 74-75.

Chapter 5 (contd)

15. **Visiting Surgeon**, Colonial Secretary Correspondence, Archives Office New South Wales 4/2500 59.1727.

16. **Sheriff**, Colonial Secretary Correspondence, Archives Office New South Wales 4/2503 61.659.

17. **Evans OS**, Colonial Secretary Correspondence, Archives Office New South Wales 4/2503 61. 426.

18. **Colonial Secretary**, Letters to Clergy, Archives Office New South Wales 4/3625 68.1421.

19. **Colonial Secretary**, Letters to Clergy, Archives Office New South Wales 4/3625 66.49.

Chapter 6.

1. *Rottnest Islander*. May 1994.
2. **Ferguson RJ**. *Rottnest Island History and Architecture*. U.W.A. Press, 1985, pp 1-5.
3. **Somerville W**. *Rottnest Island in History and Legend*. Rottnest Island Board. 1976.
4. **Green, Neville.** Broken Spears. Focus Education Services, Perth, 1984.
5. **Ibid**.
6. **Ward K. and Rigby P**. *Rottnest Island Sketchbook*. Rigby, 1969.

Chapter 6 (contd)

7. **Bentley M**. The Unwanted. **In**: Ericson R., The Brand on His Coat, U.W.A. Press, 1983, pp 222-223.

8. **Green, Neville**. Broken Spears. Focus Education Services, Perth, 1984.

Chapter 6 (contd)

9. **Lewis, Julie**. Jimmy Woods; Flying Pioneer, Fremantle Arts Centre Press, 1989.

10. **Rottnest Island Authority**, Rottnest — Links in History, Print Image Pty Ltd, 1993.

INDEX

D

E

F

M

N

O

W